BHAGAVAD
GITA

BY STEPHEN MITCHELL

POETRY
Parables and Portraits

FICTION
The Frog Prince

Meetings with the Archangel

NONFICTION
The Gospel According to Jesus

TRANSLATIONS AND ADAPTATIONS
Bhagavad Gita

Real Power: Business Lessons from the Tao Te Ching
(with James A. Autry)

Full Woman, Fleshly Apple, Hot Moon:
Selected Poems of Pablo Neruda

Genesis

Ahead of All Parting:
The Selected Poetry and Prose of Rainer Maria Rilke

A Book of Psalms

The Selected Poetry of Dan Pagis

Tao Te Ching

The Book of Job

The Selected Poetry of Yehuda Amichai
(with Chana Bloch)

The Sonnets to Orpheus

The Lay of the Love and Death of Cornet Christoph Rilke

Letters to a Young Poet

The Notebooks of Malte Laurids Brigge

The Selected Poetry of Rainer Maria Rilke

BHAGAVAD GITA

A New Translation
Stephen Mitchell

THREE RIVERS PRESS • NEW YORK

The passages on 21, 28, 202, and 206–7 are reprinted from *Tao Te Ching: A New English Version with Foreword and Notes* by Stephen Mitchell. Translation copyright © 1988 by Stephen Mitchell. Reprinted by permission of HarperCollins.

"The Message of the Gita" is reprinted from *The Collected Works of Mahatma Gandhi*, vol. XLI. Reprinted by permission of the Navajivan Trust.

Published by Three Rivers Press, New York, New York.
Member of the Crown Publishing Group, a division of Random House, Inc.
www.randomhouse.com

Three Rivers Press and the Tugboat design are registered trademarks of Random House, Inc.

Originally published in hardcover by Harmony Books, a division of Random House, Inc., in 2000.

Printed in the United States of America

Design by Barbara Sturman

LIBRARY OF CONGRESS CATALOGING-IN-PUBLICATION DATA
Bhagavadgita. English
   Bhagavad Gita: a new translation / by Stephen Mitchell.—1st ed.
      I. Mitchell, Stephen, 1943– . II. Title.
   BL1138.62.E5 2000b
   294.5′92404521—dc21   00-028286

ISBN 0-609-81034-0

10 9 8 7 6 5 4 3 2 1

First Paperback Edition

In honor of

Shri Ramana Maharshi

CONTENTS

Introduction

I

One of the best ways of entering the Bhagavad Gita is through the enthusiasm of Emerson and Thoreau, our first two American sages. Emerson mentions the Gita often in his Journals, with the greatest respect:

> It was the first of books; it was as if an empire spake to us, nothing small or unworthy but large, serene, consistent, the voice of an old intelligence which in another age & climate had pondered & thus disposed of the same questions which exercise us.

Thoreau speaks of it in awed superlatives:

> The reader is nowhere raised into and sustained in a higher, purer, or *rarer* region of thought than in the Bhagvat-Geeta. . . . Beside [it], even our Shakespeare seems sometimes youthfully green and practical merely.

What a revelation the Gita must have been for minds predisposed to its largehearted vision of the world. And what a delight to stand behind Emerson and Thoreau, reading over their shoulders as they discover this "stupendous and cosmogonal" poem in which, from the other side of the globe, across so many centuries, they can hear the voice of the absolutely genuine. Here is a kinsman, an elder brother, telling them truths that they already, though imperfectly, know, truths that are vital to them and to us all. In the Gita's wisdom, as in an ancient, clear mirror, they find that they can recognize themselves.

Souls who love God, a Sufi sheikh said a thousand years ago, "know one another by smell, like horses. Though one be in the East and the other in the West, they still feel joy and comfort in each other's talk, and one who lives in a later generation than the other is instructed and consoled by the words of his friend."

I I

Bhagavad Gita means "The Song of the Blessed One." No one knows when it was written; some scholars date it as early as the fifth century B.C.E., others as late as the first century C.E. But there is general scholarly consensus that in its original form it was an independent poem, which was later inserted into its present context, Book Six of India's national epic, the Mahabharata.

The Mahabharata is a very long poem—eight times the length of the Iliad and the Odyssey combined—that tells the story of a war between the two clans of a royal family in northern India. One clan is the Pandavas, who are portrayed as paragons of virtue; they are led by Arjuna, the hero of the Gita, and his four brothers. Opposing them are the forces of the Kauravas, their evil cousins, the hundred sons of the blind King Dhritarashtra. At the conclusion of the epic, the capital city lies in ruins and almost all the combatants have been killed.

The Gita takes place on the battlefield of Kuru at the beginning of the war. Arjuna has his charioteer, Krishna (who turns out to be God incarnate), drive him into the open space between the two armies, where he surveys the combatants. Overwhelmed with dread and pity at the imminent death of so many brave warriors—brothers, cousins, and kinsmen—he drops his weapons and refuses to fight. This is the cue for Krishna to begin his teaching about life and deathlessness, duty, nonattachment, the Self, love, spiritual practice, and the inconceivable depths of reality. The "wondrous dialogue" that fills the next seventeen chapters of the Gita is really a monologue, much of it wondrous indeed, which often keeps us dazzled and asking for more, as Arjuna does:

> for I never can tire of hearing
> your life-giving, honey-sweet words. (10.18)

The incorporation of the Gita into the Mahabharata has both its fortunate and its unfortunate aspects. It gives a thrilling dramatic immediacy to a poem that is from beginning to end didactic. Krishna and Arjuna speak about these ultimate matters not reclining at their ease, or abstracted from time and place, but between two armies about to engage in a devastating battle. We see the ranks of warriors waiting in the adrenaline rush before combat, keying up their courage, drawing their bows, glaring across the battle lines; we hear the din of the conch horns, the neighing of the horses, the thunder of the captains and the shouting. Then, suddenly, everything is still. The armies are halted in their tracks. Even the flies are caught in midair between two wingbeats. The vast moving picture of reality stops on a single frame, as in Borges's story "The Secret Miracle." The moment of the poem has expanded beyond time, and the only characters who continue, earnestly discoursing between the silent, frozen armies, are Arjuna and Krishna.

In one sense, this setting seems entirely appropriate. The subject of Krishna's teaching is, after all, a matter of the gravest urgency: the battle for authenticity, the life and death of the soul. And in all spiritual practice, the struggle against greed, hatred, and ignorance, against the ingrained selfishness that has covered over our natural luminosity, can for a long time be as ferocious as any external war. During this time even the slightest clarity or opening of the heart is a major triumph, and metaphors of victory and defeat, of conquering our enemies and overcoming fierce obstacles, seem only too accurate, as if they were straightforward description.

Yet from a clearer perspective, not only is there nothing to overcome, there is no one in particular to overcome it. Metaphors of struggle may just make the phantom dramas of the mind more solid, thus perpetuating the struggle, since even high spiritual warfare is one of the ego's self-aggrandizing dreams. After a while, all this struggle drops away naturally. The spiritually mature human being lets all things come and go without effort, without desire for any foreseen result, carried along on the current of a vast intelligence. As the great twentieth-century Hindu sage Ramana Maharshi said, "The idea that there is a goal . . . is wrong. We *are* the goal; we are always peace. To get rid of the idea that we are not peace is all that is required."

Actually, a good case can be made that the Gita's answer about war—according to which, since the war is "just," Arjuna should do his duty as a warrior, stand up like a man, and fight—is directly contradictory to the deeper lessons that Krishna teaches. How indeed can an enlightened sage, who cherishes all beings with equal compassion because he sees all beings within himself and himself within God, inflict harm on anyone, even wicked men who have launched an unjust war? This is still an open question, whatever Krishna may say. No fixed statement of the truth can apply to all circumstances, and honorable men, during every war within memory, have come to opposite conclusions about what their duty is. Gandhi, who thought of the Gita as his "eternal mother," is almost convincing when he says that the deepest spiritual awareness necessarily implies absolute nonviolence. On the other hand, I can imagine even a buddha enlisting in the war against Hitler.

Nevertheless, whether or not Arjuna should fight is at most a secondary question for the Gita. The primary question is, How should we live?

III

Or, more essentially, How should *I* live? For the Gita is a book of deeply personal instruction. When you approach it as a sacred text, you can't help standing, at first, in the place where Arjuna stands, confused and eager for illumination. Whatever intellectual or esthetic satisfaction it may provide, its purpose is to transform your life.

The Gita presents some of the most important truths of human existence in a language that is clear, memorable, and charged with emotion. It is a poem, of course, and not a systematic manual. Its method is not linear but circular and descriptive. It returns to its central point—letting go of the fruits of action—again and again, addressing not only superior students but also the great majority, who are spiritually unfocused and slow to grasp the point: "Let go."—*What does that mean?* "It means this."—*I don't get it.* "It means that."—*I still don't get it.* "Then let me paint you a picture."—*But* how *do I let go?* "Just act in this way."—*But*

I can't. "All right, then act in that way."—*But what if I can't do that either?* "All right, here's still another approach." Thus, generously, patiently, the poem guides even the least gifted of us on the path toward freedom.

One of the Gita's most effective methods of teaching is its portrait of the sage, the person who has entirely let go. This portrait is among the finest in world literature. Though not as subtle as the portrait of the Master in the Tao Te Ching, it is more easily comprehensible. Though not as profound as the wild, marvelous nonfigurative image that emerges from the dialogues of the Chinese Zen Masters, it is profound enough, and more obviously filled with the inestimable quality that we call "heart." In elaborate, loving detail, the Gita poet describes what it is like to have grown beyond the sense of a separate self, to live centered in the deathless reality at the core of our being. It is a theme he never tires of. He returns to it in almost every chapter of the poem, emphasizing now one aspect, now another, lavish with his adjectives, trying in any way he can to ignite the reader with a passionate admiration of the enlightened human being, the mature and fully realized "man of yoga," the person that all of us, men and women alike, are capable of becoming because that is who we all essentially are.

Of the various paths to self-realization—*karma yoga* (the path of action), *jñana yoga* (the path of knowledge or wisdom), *raja yoga* (the path of meditation), and *bhakti yoga* (the path of devotion or love)—the poet clearly prefers the last. But he is aware that for people of different constitutions and affinities, different paths are appropriate. When he says that one particular path is superior, his statement doesn't come at the expense of the other paths. All paths and all people are included.

Whatever their differences, the basic progression along each of these paths to no goal is similar. We begin spiritual practice by confronting, with a rude shock, the selfishness and obstinacy of the raw mind. This mind, as Arjuna says,

> is restless, unsteady,
> turbulent, wild, stubborn;
> truly, it seems to me
> as hard to master as the wind. (6.34)

Any genuine path will, with sincere practice, result in a gradual, deepening surrender of selfishness into the ultimate reality that the Gita calls the Self. Just as our primordial craving leads to all the manifold forms of our misery, letting go of our ideas about reality and our desires for particular results leads to freedom.

"Renunciation of the fruits of action," Gandhi wrote, "is the center around which the Gita is woven. It is the central sun around which devotion, knowledge, and the rest revolve like planets." This lesson is repeated over and over throughout the Gita, in seemingly endless variations. Just as the essence of

Judaism is "Love God with all your heart, and love your neighbor as yourself" (as Jesus once reminded a sympathetic scribe), the essence of Hinduism is "Let go." The two statements are, in fact, different entrances into the same truth, which is the beginning and the end of all spiritual practice.

> You have a right to your actions,
> but never to your actions' fruits.
> Act for the action's sake.
> And do not be attached to inaction.
>
> Self-possessed, resolute, act
> without any thought of results,
> open to success or failure. (2.47–48)

Or, to rephrase it in the language of the Tao Te Ching:

> Do your work, then step back.
> The only path to serenity.

The Gita's portrait of the sage may seem like an idealization. It is not. Anyone who has seen the famous photograph of Ramana Maharshi and looked into those inexpressibly beautiful eyes will know what I am talking about.

Ramana Maharshi is only the most dazzling modern instance of a long tradition in India. It is a tradition with a strongly ascetic flavor. This kind of sage barely notices his body and its needs, has no use for money or possessions, and is blithely indifferent to art, society, and sexual love, not to speak of life and death. Such dispassion may at first appear repulsive to some readers. But pure dispassion is a kind of compassion. Here is how Ramana Maharshi expresses it:

> When you truly feel equal love for all beings, when your heart has expanded so much that it embraces the whole of creation, you will certainly not feel like giving up this or that. You will simply drop off from secular life as a ripe fruit drops from the branch of a tree. You will feel that the whole world is your home.

There are other modes of enlightenment. Lao-tzu's model of the Master who is fully involved in the world and fully present in her body seems more appropriate to our Western circumstances. But the Gita's portrait is one of the classic exemplars, and it is worthy of our deepest respect.

IV

As fine as its chapters about spiritual practice and the sage are, the Gita's finest chapters are about God. The passages in which the poet has Krishna speak of himself are written at white heat, with an energy and a clarity that far surpass similar attempts in the other sacred texts of the world. These passages are sublime, crystalline, electric, stunning in their passion, their nimbleness, their density, the hugeness of their imagination, their metaphysical grace, and their readiness to cut free from rational limits. Krishna says, for example, that he is all that is. But all that is, is in him, though he is not in it. But he is the best of all that is. But he is beyond *is* and *is not*. Thus the poet keeps switching modes of reference, as our minds whirl, from one set of "I am"'s to the next.

The Gita is usually thought of as a great philosophical poem. It is that, of course. It is also an instruction manual for spiritual practice and a guide to peace of heart. But essentially it is, as its title implies, a love song to God. However powerful its thinking, its intention is not to be a treatise but a psalm. The Gita is a love song to reality, a hymn in praise of everything excellent and beautiful and brave. It is a love song to both the darkness and the light, to our own true Self in the depths of being, the core from which all the glories and horrors of the universe unfold.

The passages in which Krishna speaks about himself are so splendid that a few short examples will suffice. First, a passage of great delicacy, where the poet's love for the most fundamental elements in human life shines through his philosophical disdain for "this sad, vanishing world":

I am the taste in water,
the light in the moon and sun,
the sacred syllable *Ôm*
in the Vedas, the sound in air.

I am the fragrance in the earth,
the manliness in men, the brilliance
in fire, the life in the living,
and the abstinence in ascetics.

I am the primal seed
within all beings, Arjuna:
the wisdom of those who know,
the splendor of the high and mighty. (7.8–10)

Next, in the wonderful ninth chapter, a passage that starts
by seeing Krishna as all parts of the sacrificial rite and
expands until he is not only all parts of the cosmos but even
vaster than the category of "being":

I am the ritual and the worship,
the medicine and the mantra,
the butter burnt in the fire,
and I am the flames that consume it.

I am the father of the universe
and its mother, essence and goal
of all knowledge, the refiner, the sacred
Ôm, and the threefold Vedas.

I am the beginning and the end,
origin and dissolution,

refuge, home, true lover,
womb and imperishable seed.

I am the heat of the sun,
I hold back the rain and release it;
I am death, and the deathless,
and all that is or is not. (9.16–19)

And from chapter 8, this startling quatrain, which seems to move at the speed of light, breathless with adoration:

Meditate on the Guide,
the Giver of all, the Primordial
Poet, smaller than an atom,
unthinkable, brilliant as the sun. (8.9)

The long passages in which Krishna describes himself are extraordinarily moving. They keep brimming over with love and boldness. Krishna's first-person pronoun is a resplendent act of the human imagination: it is the poet himself speaking *as* God so that he can speak *about* God. His love here is so intense and intimate that the reader must step into the words to see that every "I" is really a "you."

One element of Krishna's attitude that will impress even the most casual reader is his tolerance and inclusiveness. Even those who don't know him are held in the truly magnificent embrace of the following quatrain:

However men try to reach me,
I return their love with my love;
whatever path they may travel,
it leads to me in the end. (4.11)

And, at least in the first two-thirds of the poem, Krishna's largehearted attitude toward the wicked reminds us of Jesus's God, who "makes his sun rise on the wicked and on the good, and sends rain to the righteous and to the unrighteous":

Even the heartless criminal,
if he loves me with all his heart,
will certainly grow into sainthood
as he moves toward me on this path.

Quickly that man becomes pure,
his heart finds eternal peace.
Arjuna, no one who truly
loves me will ever be lost.

All those who love and trust me,
even the lowest of the low —
prostitutes, beggars, slaves —
will attain the ultimate goal. (9.30–32)

The climax of the Gita is its eleventh chapter, in which Krishna appears to Arjuna in his supreme form. It is a terrifying theophany, a glimpse into a level of reality that is more than the ordinary mind can bear. Arjuna sees

> the whole universe
> enfolded, with its countless billions
> of life-forms, gathered together
> in the body of the God of gods. (11.13)

Krishna dazzles his sight, blazing

> in the measureless, massive, sun-flame
> splendor of [his] radiant form. (11.17)

This is a vision of pure energy, which does not discriminate between good and evil, creation and destruction. No wonder it entered modern history through the story of Robert Oppenheimer's response to the first atomic explosion at Alamogordo on July 16, 1945. What other image from world literature could have been so uncannily right for that occasion?

> If a thousand suns were to rise
> and stand in the noon sky, blazing,
> such brilliance would be like the fierce
> brilliance of that mighty Self. (11.12)

As the bomb exploded, Oppenheimer thought of another, later verse:

I am death, shatterer of worlds,
annihilating all things. (11.32)

The appropriateness of this reference, too, is uncanny.

The vision of God as elemental undifferentiated energy is an aspect of the truth, a difficult aspect for many Western readers to understand or accept. There is little precedent for it in our own scriptures, which split the universe into good and evil and place God solely on the side of the good. The only exceptions are the Voice from the Whirlwind at the end of the Book of Job and a single, hair-raising verse from Second Isaiah: "I form the light, and create darkness; I make peace, and create evil: I the Lord do all these things."

Realizing that both the creative and the destructive issue from the infinite intelligence of the universe allows us to accept the whole of reality:

> The Tao doesn't take sides;
> it gives birth to both good and evil.
> The Master doesn't take sides;
> she welcomes both saints and sinners.

Arjuna is not yet at this stage; in fact, he is at the very beginning of his spiritual practice. The vision of the whole terrifies him; his blood chills; the hair stands up on his flesh. He has the presence of mind to sing an ecstatic paean to God's infinite darkness-and-light-embracing power. But then dread overwhelms him, he begs for the vision to be taken away, and Krishna resumes his "kind and beautiful" human form.

The eleventh chapter of the Gita is one of the great moments in world literature. The only fitting sequel to it in the rest of the poem would be pure silence.

V

The most profound sacred texts have a way of self-destructing. They undermine their own authority and glee-fully hoist themselves with their own petard. Because they don't confuse what they are with what they are about, they encourage us to see them as, in the end, disposable.

> As unnecessary as a well is
> to a village on the banks of a river,
> so unnecessary are all scriptures
> to someone who has seen the truth. (2.46)

> When your understanding has passed
> beyond the thicket of delusions,
> there is nothing you need to learn
> from even the most sacred scripture.

> Indifferent to scriptures, your mind
> stands by itself, unmoving,
> absorbed in deep meditation.
> This is the essence of yoga. (2.52–53)

We need to take these sacred texts with ultimate seriousness. But the tao that can be told is not the eternal Tao. If we take them too seriously, they become obstacles rather than means of liberation.

The healthiest way to begin reading and absorbing a text like the Bhagavad Gita is to understand that ultimately it has nothing to teach. Everything essential that it points to—what we call wisdom or radiance or peace—is already present inside us. Once we have practiced meditation sincerely and seen layer after layer of the inauthentic fall away, we come to a place where dualities such as sacred and profane, spiritual and unspiritual, fall away as well.

> Zen Master Hsueh-feng asked a monk where he had come from. The monk said, "From the Monastery of Spiritual Light."
>
> The Master said, "In the daytime, we have sunlight; in the evening, we have lamplight. What is spiritual light?"
>
> The monk couldn't answer.
>
> The Master said, "Sunlight. Lamplight."

In that place, God is the ground we walk on, the food we eat, and the gratitude we express, to no one in particular, as naturally as breathing.

About the Translation

B ecause my knowledge of Sanskrit is rudimentary, I depended on two principal guides to take me by the hand and lead me through the intricacies of the text. Winthrop Sargeant's interlinear translation with running vocabulary and grammatical analysis (*The Bhagavad Gita*, SUNY Press, 1984) did all the busywork for me and made my first draft a relative breeze. The meticulous line-by-line commentary by Robert N. Minor (*Bhagavad-Gita: An Exegetical Commentary*, South Asia Books, 1982) clarified my understanding of the Gita's use of a number of difficult terms, most notably *brahman*, and shaped my interpretation of many dozens of verses. I am deeply indebted to both of them.

I also consulted in detail a number of other translations: the literal ones by Franklin Edgerton, S. Radhakrishnan, and R. C. Zaehner, the mostly literal translation by Barbara Stoler Miller, and the interpretive, paraphrastic versions by Eknath Easwaran, Swami Phabhavananda and Christopher Isherwood, and Shri Purohit Swami. I learned from each of them and occasionally borrowed a word or a phrase that seemed just right.

The main problem in translating the Gita—at least, *my* main problem —was finding the right verse form in English.

The Gita is written in syllabic verse. Its normal meter, the *śloka*, divides into four lines of eight syllables each, with certain prescribed alternations of long and short syllables; the closest analogy in Western literature is classical Greek or Latin verse. (There is also a longer meter called the *triṣṭubh*, which crops up at odd intervals. Though according to the traditional view this meter is used in the Gita for verses of greater intensity, some of the most intense passages in the Gita are written in the *śloka* meter, and the variation between *triṣṭubh* and *śloka* is fairly arbitrary.)

What seemed to me essential was finding a line that had the dignity of formal verse, yet was free and supple enough to sound like natural speech. For many years I thought that if I ever translated the Gita, I would use a four-beat line to re-create the eight syllables of the Sanskrit. But when I finally began, I found that the tetrameter—like its longer cousin, the ill-fated English hexameter—tends to break apart into two shorter lines; and even when it succeeds, it often carries with it the resonance of Old English verse, which would have been jarring here. The form that I came to use is a loose trimeter quatrain.* I have worked hard to keep the rhythms from sounding too regular and to vary them so that no two consecutive lines have the identical rhythm.

*Except in the expository prologue—chapter 1 and the beginning of chapter 2—where prose seemed more appropriate.

Certain Sanskrit words that are central concepts in the Gita seemed better left untranslated. *Yoga,* for example, has by now become a comfortable English word, though in its more limited sense of physical or hatha yoga. In the Gita, it has a wide range of meanings: path, practice, discipline, and meditation, among others. Restricting it to "discipline" alone would be an impoverishment, I thought; besides, how could one expect the reader to keep a straight face at the image of Krishna as the "Lord of Discipline"? I have also left untranslated the Sanskrit term *guna* (strand or quality), along with *sattva, rajas,* and *tamas.* Attempts to find English equivalents for such concepts have been uniformly unsuccessful and confuse more than they clarify. It is like translating *Tao* as "the Way," or *yin* and *yang* as "darkness and light": accurate up to a point, but limiting. The meaning of these terms becomes fairly clear from the context, especially after chapter 14. But since they occur a number of times earlier in the Gita, it might be helpful to refer to the following brief explanation by Winthrop Sargeant:

> The three *gunas*—*sattva,* or illumination and truth,
> *rajas,* or passion and desire, and *tamas,* or darkness,
> sloth, and dullness—were originally thought, by the
> Samkhya philosophers who first identified and named
> them, to be substances. Later they became attributes
> of the psyche. *Sattva* has been equated with essence,

rajas with energy, and *tamas* with mass. According to still another interpretation, *sattva* is intelligence, *rajas* is movement, and *tamas* is obstruction. The word *guṇa* means "strand," "thread," or "rope," and *prakṛti*, or material nature, is conceived as a cord woven from the three *guṇas*. They chain down the soul to thought and matter. They can exist in different proportions in a single being, determining his mental outlook and his actions. A man whose nature is dominated by *sattva* will be clear-thinking, radiant, and truthful. A man whose nature is dominated by *rajas* will be passionate, quick to anger, and greedy. A man whose nature is dominated by *tamas* will be stupid, lazy, and stubborn. But most men will be found to have elements of *guṇas* different from their dominating ones, i.e., to be motivated by a combination of *guṇas*. The aim of the upward-reaching *atman*, or Self, is to transcend the *guṇas*, break free of their bondage, and attain liberation. (*The Bhagavad Gita*, 331)

One last item: the reader will notice that in the following pages wisdom seems to be a male prerogative, whereas in my version of the Tao Te Ching I have been careful to portray the Master as alternately "she" and "he." But in Lao-tzu's infinitely open, fluid, and gender-generous sense of the world, wisdom belongs to us all; we are urged to "know the male, yet keep to the female"; and the Tao itself is called the Mysterious Woman or Great Mother. The poet of the Gita, on the other hand, was writing mostly for priests (brahmins) and warriors; according to his cultural preconceptions, rebirth as a woman is a stroke of rotten karma, which can indeed be overcome, but only with wholehearted devotion. (The literal meaning of 9.32 is "Those who take refuge in me, Arjuna, / even if they are born in evil wombs / as women or laborers or servants, / also reach the supreme goal.") Given this mind-set, it would have been too much of a distortion for me to call the sage "the wise woman" or even "the wise man or woman." I hope that women who read these pages will forgive this particular limitation of the Gita's consciousness and realize that, with its spirit if not always with its words, it is pointing all of us to the essential truth.

NOTE

Stanza numbers printed within brackets in the top
outer margins of the following pages refer to the
Sanskrit text; they don't always correspond to the
stanzas of this translation.

BHAGAVAD
GITA

Chapter 1

ARJUNA'S DESPAIR

KING DHRITARASHTRA SAID:

*In the field of righteousness, the field of Kuru, tell
me, Sanjaya, what happened when my army and
the Pandavas faced each other, eager for battle?*

THE POET SANJAYA SAID:

*Seeing the ranks of the Pandavas' forces, Prince
Duryodhana approached his teacher, Drona,
and spoke these words: "Look at this great army,
led by the son of Drupada, your worthy pupil.
Many great warriors stand ready to do battle,
many great archers, men as formidable as Bhima
and Arjuna: Yuyudhana, Virata, the mighty
Drupada, Dhrishtaketu, Chekitana, the heroic
king of Benares, Purujit, Kuntibhoja, Shaibya
that bull among men, bold Yudhamanyu,*

Uttamaujas famous for his courage, the son of Subhadra,
and the sons of Draupadi, all of them great warriors. Now,
most honored of priests, look at the great men on our side,
the leaders of my army: you, first of all, then Bhishma,
Karna, the always-victorious Kripa, Ashvatthama,
Vikarna, the son of Somadatta, and many other heroes—
all of them skilled in war and armed with many kinds
of weapons—who are risking their lives for my sake.
Limitless is this army of ours, led by Bhishma; but their
army, led by Bhima, is limited. Wherever the battle
moves, all of you must stand firm and make sure that
Bhishma is well protected."

Then Bhishma, the aged grandfather of the Kurus,
roared his lion's roar and blew a powerful blast on his
conch horn, and Duryodhana's heart leapt with joy.
Immediately all the conches blared, and the kettledrums,
cymbals, trumpets, and drums: a deafening clamor.
Standing in their great chariot yoked with white horses,
Krishna and Arjuna blew their celestial conches: Krishna
blew the conch called "Won from the Demon Panchajanya";
Arjuna blew "God Given"; ferocious, wolf-bellied Bhima
blew the mighty conch called "King Paundra"; Prince
Yudhishthira blew "Unending Victory"; Nakula and his
twin, Sahadeva, blew "Great Noise" and "Jewel Bracelet";
the king of Benares that superb archer, the great warrior
Shikhandi, Dhrishtadyumna, Virata, the unconquerable

Satyaki, Drupada, Draupadi's sons, the huge-armed
Abhimanyu—all of them, O King, blew their conches at
once. The uproar tore through the hearts of Dhritarashtra's
men and echoed throughout heaven and earth.

Then Arjuna, looking at the battle ranks of Dhritarashtra's men, raised his bow as the weapons were about
to clash, and said to Krishna, "Drive my chariot and stop
between the two armies, so that I can see these warriors
whom I am about to fight, drawn up and eager for battle.
I want to look at the men gathered here ready to do
battle service for Dhritarashtra's evil-minded son."

After Arjuna had spoken, Krishna drove the splendid
chariot and brought it to a halt midway between the two
armies. Facing Bhishma, Drona, and the other great kings,
he said: "Look, Arjuna. From here you can see all the
Kurus who are gathered to do battle."

Arjuna saw them standing there: fathers, grandfathers,
teachers, uncles, brothers, sons, grandsons, fathers-in-law,
and friends, kinsmen on both sides, each side arrayed
against the other. In despair, overwhelmed with pity, he
said: "As I see my own kinsmen, gathered here, eager to
fight, my legs weaken, my mouth dries, my body trembles,
my hair stands on end, my skin burns, the bow Gandiva
drops from my hand, I am beside myself, my mind reels.
I see evil omens, Krishna; no good can come from killing
my own kinsmen in battle. I have no desire for victory or

*for the pleasures of kingship. What good is kingship, or
happiness, or life itself, when those for whose sake we
desire them—teachers, fathers, sons, grandfathers, uncles,
fathers-in-law, grandsons, brothers-in-law, and other kinsmen—stand here in battle ranks, ready to give up their
fortunes and their lives? Though they want to kill me, I
have no desire to kill them, not even for the kingship of the
three worlds, let alone for that of the earth. What joy
would we have in killing Dhritarashtra's men? Evil will
cling to us if we kill them, even though they are the aggres-
sors. And it would be unworthy of us to kill our own kinsmen. How could we be happy if we did? Because their
minds are overpowered by greed, they see no harm in
destroying the family, no crime in treachery to friends.
But we should know better, Krishna: clearly seeing the
harm caused by the destruction of the family, we should
turn back from this evil. When the family is destroyed,
the ancient laws of family duty cease; when law ceases,
lawlessness overwhelms the family; when lawlessness overwhelms the women of the family, they become corrupted;
when women are corrupted, the intermixture of castes is
the inevitable result. Intermixture of castes drags down to
hell both those who destroy the family and the family itself;
the spirits of the ancestors fall, deprived of their offerings
of rice and water. Such are the evils caused by those who
destroy the family: because of the intermixture of castes,*

caste duties are obliterated and the permanent duties of the family as well. We have often heard, Krishna, that men whose family duties have been obliterated must live in hell forever. Alas! We are about to commit a great evil by killing our own kinsmen, because of our greed for the pleasures of kingship. It would be better if Dhritarashtra's men killed me in battle, unarmed and unresisting."

Having spoken these words, Arjuna sank down into the chariot and dropped his arrows and bow, his mind heavy with grief.

Chapter 2

THE PRACTICE OF YOGA

As Arjuna sat there, overwhelmed with pity, desperate, tears streaming from his eyes, Krishna spoke these words to him: "Why this timidity, Arjuna, at a time of crisis? It is unworthy of a noble mind; it is shameful and does not lead to heaven. This cowardice is beneath you, Arjuna; do not give in to it. Shake off your weakness. Stand up now like a man."

Arjuna said: "When the battle begins, how can I shoot arrows through Bhishma and Drona, who deserve my reverence? It would be better to spend the rest of my life as a pauper, begging for food, than to kill these honored teachers. If I killed them, all my earthly pleasures would be smeared with blood. And we do not know which is worse, winning this battle or losing it, since if

*we kill Dhritarashtra's men we will not wish to remain
alive. I am weighed down by pity, Krishna; my mind is
utterly confused. Tell me where my duty lies, which path
I should take. I am your pupil; I beg you for your instruction. For I cannot imagine how any victory—even if I
were to gain the kingship of the whole earth or of all
the gods in heaven—could drive away this grief that is
withering my senses."*

*Having spoken thus to Krishna, Arjuna said: "I will
not fight," and fell silent.*

*As Arjuna sat there, downcast, between the two
armies, Krishna smiled at him, then spoke these words.*

THE BLESSED LORD SAID:

Although you mean well, Arjuna,
your sorrow is sheer delusion.
Wise men do not grieve
for the dead or for the living.

Never was there a time
when I did not exist, or you,
or these kings; nor will there come
a time when we cease to be.

Just as, in this body, the Self
passes through childhood, youth,
and old age, so after death
it passes to another body.

Physical sensations—cold
and heat, pleasure and pain—
are transient: they come and go;
so bear them patiently, Arjuna.

Only the man who is unmoved
by any sensations, the wise man
indifferent to pleasure, to pain,
is fit for becoming deathless.

Nonbeing can never be;
being can never not be.
Both these statements are obvious
to those who have seen the truth.

The presence that pervades the universe
is imperishable, unchanging,
beyond both *is* and *is not:*
how could it ever vanish?

These bodies come to an end;
but that vast embodied Self
is ageless, fathomless, eternal.
Therefore you must fight, Arjuna.

If you think that this Self can kill
or think that it can be killed,
you do not well understand
reality's subtle ways.

It never was born; coming
to be, it will never *not* be.
Birthless, primordial, it does not
die when the body dies.

Knowing that it is eternal,
unborn, beyond destruction,
how could you ever kill?
And whom could you kill, Arjuna?

Just as you throw out used clothes
and put on other clothes, new ones,
the Self discards its used bodies
and puts on others that are new.

The sharpest sword will not pierce it;
the hottest flame will not singe it;
water will not make it moist;
wind will not cause it to wither.

It cannot be pierced or singed,
moistened or withered; it is vast,
perfect and all-pervading,
calm, immovable, timeless.

It is called the Inconceivable,
the Unmanifest, the Unchanging.
If you understand it in this way,
you have no reason for your sorrow.

Even if you think that the Self
is perpetually born and perpetually
dies—even then, Arjuna,
you have no reason for your sorrow.

Death is certain for the born;
for the dead, rebirth is certain.
Since both cannot be avoided,
you have no reason for your sorrow.

Before birth, beings are unmanifest;
between birth and death, manifest;
at death, unmanifest again.
What cause for grief in all this?

Some perceive it directly
in all its awesomeness; others
speak of it with wonder; others
hear of it and never know it.

This Self who dwells in the body
is inviolable, forever;
therefore you have no cause to grieve
for any being, Arjuna.

Know what your duty is
and do it without hesitation.
For a warrior, there is nothing better
than a battle that duty enjoins.

Blessed are warriors who are given
the chance of a battle like this,
which calls them to do what is right
and opens the gates of heaven.

But if you refuse the call

to a righteous war, and shrink from

what duty and honor dictate,

you will bring down ruin on your head.

Decent men, for all time,

will talk about your disgrace;

and disgrace, for a man of honor,

is a fate far worse than death.

These great heroes will think

that fear has driven you from battle;

all those who once esteemed you

will think of you with contempt.

And your enemies will sneer and mock you:

"The mighty Arjuna, that brave man—

he slunk from the field like a dog."

What deeper shame could there be?

If you are killed, you gain heaven;

triumph, and you gain the earth.

Therefore stand up, Arjuna;

steady your mind to fight.

Indifferent to gain or loss,
to victory or defeat,
prepare yourself for the battle
and do not succumb to sin.

This is philosophy's wisdom;
now hear the wisdom of yoga.
Armed with this understanding,
you will shatter your karmic bonds.

On this path no effort is wasted,
no gain is ever reversed;
even a little of this practice
will shelter you from great sorrow.

Resolute understanding
is single pointed, Arjuna;
but the thoughts of the irresolute
are many-branched and endless.

Foolish men talk of religion
in cheap, sentimental words,
leaning on the scriptures: "God
speaks here, and speaks here alone."

Driven by desire for pleasure
and power, caught up in ritual,
they strive to gain heaven; but rebirth
is the only result of their striving.

They are lured by their own desires,
besotted by the scriptures' words;
their minds have not been made clear
by the practice of meditation.

The scriptures dwell in duality.
Be beyond all opposites, Arjuna:
anchored in the real, and free
from all thoughts of wealth and comfort.

As unnecessary as a well is
to a village on the banks of a river,
so unnecessary are all scriptures
to someone who has seen the truth.

You have a right to your actions,
but never to your actions' fruits.
Act for the action's sake.
And do not be attached to inaction.

Self-possessed, resolute, act
without any thought of results,
open to success or failure.
This equanimity is yoga.

Action is far inferior
to the yoga of insight, Arjuna.
Pitiful are those who, acting,
are attached to their action's fruits.

The wise man lets go of all
results, whether good or bad,
and is focused on the action alone.
Yoga is skill in actions.

The wise man whose insight is firm,
relinquishing the fruits of action,
is freed from the bondage of rebirth
and attains the place beyond sorrow.

When your understanding has passed
beyond the thicket of delusions,
there is nothing you need to learn
from even the most sacred scripture.

Indifferent to scriptures, your mind
stands by itself, unmoving,
absorbed in deep meditation.
This is the essence of yoga.

ARJUNA SAID:

How would you describe the man
whose wisdom is steadfast, Krishna?
How does the wise man speak?
How does he sit, stand, walk?

THE BLESSED LORD SAID:

When a man gives up all desires
that emerge from the mind, and rests
contented in the Self by the Self,
he is called a man of firm wisdom.

He whose mind is untroubled
by any misfortune, whose craving
for pleasures has disappeared,
who is free from greed, fear, anger,

who is unattached to all things,
who neither grieves nor rejoices
if good or if bad things happen —
that man is a man of firm wisdom.

Having drawn back all his senses
from the objects of sense, as a tortoise
draws back into its shell,
that man is a man of firm wisdom.

Sense-objects fade for the abstinent,
yet the craving for them continues;
but even the craving vanishes
for someone who has seen the truth.

At first, although he continually
tries to subdue them, the turbulent
senses tear at his mind
and violently carry it away.

Restraining the senses, disciplined,
he should focus his whole mind on me;
when the senses are in his control,
that man is a man of firm wisdom.

If a man keeps dwelling on sense-objects,
attachment to them arises;
from attachment, desire flares up;
from desire, anger is born;

from anger, confusion follows;
from confusion, weakness of memory;
weak memory — weak understanding;
weak understanding — ruin.

But the man who is self-controlled,
who meets the objects of the senses
with neither craving nor aversion,
will attain serenity at last.

In serenity, all his sorrows
disappear at once, forever;
when his heart has become serene,
his understanding is steadfast.

The undisciplined have no wisdom,
no one-pointed concentration;
with no concentration, no peace;
with no peace, where can joy be?

When the mind constantly runs
after the wandering senses,
it drives away wisdom, like the wind
blowing a ship off course.

And so, Arjuna, when someone
is able to withdraw his senses
from every object of sensation,
that man is a man of firm wisdom.

In the night of all beings, the wise man
sees only the radiance of the Self;
but the sense-world where all beings wake,
for him is as dark as night.

The man whom desires enter
as rivers flow into the sea,
filled yet always unmoving—
that man finds perfect peace.

Abandoning all desires,
acting without craving, free
from all thoughts of "I" and "mine,"
that man finds utter peace.

This is the divine state, Arjuna.
Absorbed in it, everywhere, always,
even at the moment of death,
he vanishes, into God's bliss.

Chapter 3

THE YOGA OF ACTION

ARJUNA SAID:

If you think that understanding
is superior to action, Krishna,
why do you keep on urging me
to engage in this savage act?

With words that seem inconsistent,
your teaching has bewildered my mind.
Tell me: what must I do
to arrive at the highest good?

THE BLESSED LORD SAID:

In this world there are two main paths:
the yoga of understanding,
for contemplative men; and for men
who are active, the yoga of action.

Not by avoiding actions
does a man gain freedom from action,
and not by renunciation
alone, can he reach the goal.

No one, not even for an instant,
can exist without acting; all beings
are compelled, however unwilling,
by the three strands of Nature called *gunas*.

He who controls his actions
but lets his mind dwell on sense-objects
is deluding himself and spoiling
his search for the deepest truth.

The superior man is he
whose mind can control his senses;
with no attachment to results,
he engages in the yoga of action.

Do any actions you *must* do,
since action is better than inaction;
even the existence of your body
depends on necessary actions.

The whole world becomes a slave
to its own activity, Arjuna;
if you want to be truly free,
perform all actions as worship.

The Lord of Creatures formed worship
together with mankind, and said:
"By worship you will always be fruitful
and your wishes will be fulfilled.

"By worship you will nourish the gods
and the gods will nourish you in turn;
by nourishing one another
you assure the well-being of all.

"Nourished by your worship, the gods
will grant whatever you desire;
but he who accepts their gifts
and gives nothing back, is a thief."

Good men are released from their sins
when they eat food offered in worship;
but the wicked devour their own evil
when they cook for themselves alone.

Beings arise from food;
food arises from rain;
rain arises from worship;
worship, from ritual action;

ritual action, from God;
God, from the deathless Self.
Thus, the all-present God
requires the worship of men.

He who fails to keep turning
the wheel thus set in motion
has damaged the working of the world
and has wasted his life, Arjuna.

But the man who delights in the Self,
who feels pure contentment and finds
perfect peace in the Self—
for him, there is no need to act.

He has nothing to achieve by action,
nothing to gain by inaction,
nor does he depend on any
person outside himself.

Without concern for results,
perform the necessary action;
surrendering all attachments,
accomplish life's highest good.

Only by selfless action
did Janaka and other wise kings
govern, and thus assure
the well-being of the whole world.

Whatever a great man does
ordinary people will do;
whatever standard he sets
everyone else will follow.

In all the three worlds, Arjuna,
there is nothing I need to do,
nothing I must attain;
and yet I engage in action.

For if I were to refrain
from my tireless, continual action,
mankind would follow my example
and would also not act, Arjuna.

If I stopped acting, these worlds
would plunge into ruin; chaos
would overpower all beings;
mankind would be destroyed.

Though the unwise cling to their actions,
watching for results, the wise
are free of attachments, and act
for the well-being of the whole world.

The wise man does not unsettle
the minds of the ignorant; quietly
acting in the spirit of yoga,
he inspires them to do the same.

Actions are really performed
by the working of the three *gunas;*
but a man deluded by the I-sense
imagines, "I am the doer."

The wise man knows that when objects
act on the senses, it is merely
the *gunas* acting on the *gunas;*
thus, he is unattached.

Deluded by the *gunas,* men grow
attached to the *gunas'* actions;
the insightful should not disturb
the minds of these foolish men.

Performing all actions for my sake,
desireless, absorbed in the Self,
indifferent to "I" and "mine,"
let go of your grief, and fight!

Men who constantly practice
this teaching of mine, Arjuna,
who trust it with all their heart,
are freed from the bondage of actions.

But those who, mistrustful, half-hearted,
fail to practice my teaching,
wander in the darkness, lost,
stupefied by delusion.

Even the wise man acts
in accordance with his inner nature.
All beings follow their nature.
What good can repression do?

Craving and aversion arise
when the senses encounter sense-objects.
Do not fall prey to these two
brigands blocking your path.

It is better to do your own duty
badly, than to perfectly do
another's; you are safe from harm
when you do what you should be doing.

ARJUNA SAID:

What is it that drives a man
to an evil action, Krishna,
even against his will,
as if some force made him do it?

THE BLESSED LORD SAID:

That force is desire, it is anger,
arising from the *guna* called *rajas;*
deadly and all-devouring,
that is the enemy here.

As a fire is obscured by smoke,
as a mirror is covered by dust,
as a fetus is wrapped in its membrane,
so wisdom is obscured by desire.

Wisdom is destroyed, Arjuna,
by the constant enemy of the wise,
which, flaring up as desire,
blazes with insatiable flames.

Desire dwells in the senses,
the mind, and the understanding;
in all these it obscures wisdom
and perplexes the embodied Self.

Therefore you must first control
your senses, Arjuna; then
destroy this evil that prevents you
from ever knowing the truth.

Men say that the senses are strong.
But the mind is stronger than the senses;
the understanding is stronger
than the mind; and strongest is the Self.

Knowing the Self, sustaining
the self by the Self, Arjuna,
kill the difficult-to-conquer
enemy called desire.

Chapter 4

THE YOGA OF WISDOM

THE BLESSED LORD SAID:

I taught this imperishable doctrine
to Vivasvat, god of the sun,
more than a hundred billion
years ago; Vivasvat told it

to Manu, father of humans;
Manu to King Ikshvaku;
transmitted from one generation
to the next, it was known for eons

to all the primeval wise men,
the seers and philosopher-kings.
But over the dwindling ages
the doctrine has been lost, Arjuna.

This is the ancient doctrine
that I have taught you today,
since you are my devotee and friend.
This is the innermost doctrine.

ARJUNA SAID:

But you were born countless eons
later than the god of the sun.
How, then, is it possible
that you taught this doctrine to him?

THE BLESSED LORD SAID:

Many times I have been born,
and many times you have, also.
All these lives I remember;
you recall only this one.

Although I am unborn, deathless,
the infinite Lord of all beings,
through my own wondrous power
I come into finite form.

Whenever righteousness falters

and chaos threatens to prevail,

I take on a human body

and manifest myself on earth.

In order to protect the good,

to destroy the doers of evil,

to ensure the triumph of righteousness,

in every age I am born.

Whoever knows, profoundly,

my divine presence on earth

is not reborn when he leaves

the body, but comes to me.

Released from greed, fear, anger,

absorbed in me and made pure

by the practice of wisdom, many

have attained my own state of being.

However men try to reach me,

I return their love with my love;

whatever path they may travel,

it leads to me in the end.

Wishing success in their actions,
men sacrifice to the gods,
for ritual can bring success
quickly in the world of men.

I founded the four-caste system
with the *gunas* appropriate to each;
although I did this, know
that I am the eternal non-doer.

Actions cannot defile me,
since I am indifferent to results;
all those who understand this
will not be bound by their actions.

This is how actions were done
by the ancient seekers of freedom;
follow their example: act,
surrendering the fruits of action.

What are action and inaction?
This matter confuses even
wise men; so I will teach you
and free you from any harm.

You must realize what action is,
what wrong action and inaction are
as well. The true nature of action
is profound, and difficult to fathom.

He who can see inaction
in the midst of action, and action
in the midst of inaction, is wise
and can act in the spirit of yoga.

With no desire for success,
no anxiety about failure,
indifferent to results, he burns up
his actions in the fire of wisdom.

Surrendering all thoughts of outcome,
unperturbed, self-reliant,
he does nothing at all, even
when fully engaged in actions.

There is nothing that he expects,
nothing that he fears. Serene,
free from possessions, untainted,
acting with the body alone,

content with whatever happens,
unattached to pleasure or pain,
success or failure, he acts
and is never bound by his action.

When a man has let go of attachments,
when his mind is rooted in wisdom,
everything he does is worship
and his actions all melt away.

God is the offering, God
is the offered, poured out by God;
God is attained by all those
who see God in every action.

Some men of yoga pray
to the gods, and make this their worship;
some offer worship by worship
itself, in the fire of God;

others offer their senses
in the fire of self-abnegation;
others offer the senses'
objects, in the fire of the senses;

others offer all actions
of the senses and of the breath
in the fire —kindled by wisdom —
of the yoga of self-restraint.

Some offer wealth, austerities,
their practice of yoga; others—
ascetics—offer their studies
of the scriptures, and wisdom itself;

others, intent on control
of their vital forces, offer
their in-breath into their out-breath
or their out-breath into their in-breath;

others, while fasting, offer
their in-breath into their in-breath.
All these understand worship;
by worship they are cleansed of sin.

Partaking of the essence of worship,
forever they are freed of themselves;
but non-worshipers cannot be happy
in this world or any other.

Thus, many forms of worship
may lead to freedom, Arjuna.
All these are born of action.
When you know this, you will be free.

Better than any ritual
is the worship achieved through wisdom;
wisdom is the final goal
of every action, Arjuna.

Find a wise teacher, honor him,
ask him your questions, serve him;
someone who has seen the truth
will guide you on the path to wisdom.

When you realize it, you will never
fall back into delusion;
knowing it, you see all beings
in yourself, and yourself in me.

Even if you were the most evil
of evildoers, Arjuna,
wisdom is the boat that would carry you
across the sea of all sin.

Just as firewood is turned
to ashes in the flames of a fire,
all actions are turned to ashes
in wisdom's refining flames.

Nothing in the world can purify
as powerfully as wisdom;
practiced in yoga, you will find
this wisdom within yourself.

Resolute, restraining his senses,
the man of faith becomes wise;
once he attains true wisdom,
he soon attains perfect peace.

Ignorant men without faith
are easily mired in doubt;
they can never be truly happy
in this world or the world beyond.

A man is not bound by action
who renounces action through yoga,
who concentrates on the Self,
and whose doubt is cut off by wisdom.

Therefore, with the sword of wisdom
cut off this doubt in your heart;
follow the path of selfless
action; stand up, Arjuna!

Chapter 5

THE YOGA OF
RENUNCIATION

ARJUNA SAID:

You have praised both renunciation
and the yoga of action, Krishna.
Tell me now: of these two,
which is the better path?

THE BLESSED LORD SAID:

Renunciation and yoga
both lead to the ultimate good;
but of the two paths, Arjuna,
yoga is the more direct.

The true renunciate neither
desires things nor avoids them;
indifferent to pleasure and pain,
he is easily freed from all bondage.

Fools say that knowledge and yoga
are separate, but the wise do not.
When you practice one of them deeply,
you gain the rewards of both.

The state reached by true knowledge
is reached by yoga as well.
Both paths lead to the Self;
both lead to selfless action.

It is hard to renounce all action
without engaging in action;
the sage, wholehearted in the yoga
of action, soon attains freedom.

Wholehearted, purified, mastering
body and mind, his self
becomes the self of all beings;
he is unstained by anything he does.

The man who has seen the truth
thinks, "I am not the doer"
at all times—when he sees, hears, touches,
when he smells, eats, walks, sleeps, breathes,

when he defecates, talks, or takes hold,
when he opens his eyes or shuts them:
at all times he thinks, "This is merely
sense-objects acting on the senses."

Offering his actions to God,
he is free of all action; sin
rolls off him, as drops of water
roll off a lotus leaf.

Surrendering attachment, the sage
performs all actions—with his body,
his mind, and his understanding—
only to make himself pure.

The resolute in yoga surrender
results, and gain perfect peace;
the irresolute, attached to results,
are bound by everything they do.

Calmly renouncing all actions,
the embodied Self dwells at ease
as lord of the nine-gated city,
not acting, not causing action.

It does not create the means
of action, or the action itself,
or the union of result and action:
all these arise from Nature.

Nor does it partake of anyone's
virtuous or evil actions.
When knowledge of the Self is obscured
by ignorance, men act badly.

But when ignorance is completely
destroyed, then the light of wisdom
shines like the midday sun
and illumines what is supreme.

Contemplating That, inspired
and rooted and absorbed in That,
men reach the state of true freedom
from which there is no rebirth.

Wise men regard all beings
as equal: a learned priest,
a cow, an elephant, a rat,
or a filthy, rat-eating outcaste.

Freed from the endless cycle
of birth and death, they can act
impartially toward all beings,
since to them all beings are the same.

They do not rejoice in good fortune;
they do not lament at bad fortune;
lucid, with minds unshaken,
they remain within what is real.

A man unattached to sensations,
who finds fulfillment in the Self,
whose mind has become pure freedom,
attains an imperishable joy.

Pleasures from external objects
are wombs of suffering, Arjuna.
They have their beginnings and their ends;
no wise man seeks joy among them.

The man of yoga who is able
to overcome, here on earth,
the turmoil of desire and anger—
that man is truly happy.

He who finds peace and joy
and radiance within himself—
that man becomes one with God
and vanishes into God's bliss.

The wise man, cleansed of his sins,
who has cut off all separation,
who delights in the welfare of all beings,
vanishes into God's bliss.

He who controls his mind
and has cut off desire and anger
realizes the Self; he knows
that God's bliss is nearer than near.

Closing his eyes, his vision
focused between the eyebrows,
making the in-breath and the out-breath
equal as they pass through his nostrils,

he controls his senses and his mind,
intent upon liberation;
when desire, fear, and anger have left him,
that man is forever free.

Knowing me as the enjoyer
of all worship, the Lord of all worlds,
the dearest friend of all beings,
that man gains perfect peace.

Chapter 6

THE YOGA OF MEDITATION

THE BLESSED LORD SAID:

He who performs his duty
with no concern for results
is the true man of yoga—not
he who refrains from action.

Know that right action itself
is renunciation, Arjuna;
in the yoga of action, you first
renounce your own selfish will.

For the man who wishes to mature,
the yoga of action is the path;
for the man already mature,
serenity is the path.

When a man has become unattached
to sense-objects or to actions,
renouncing his own selfish will,
then he is mature in yoga.

He should lift up the self by the Self
and not sink into the selfish;
for the self is the only friend
of the Self, and its only foe.

The self is a friend for him
who masters himself by the Self;
but for him who is not self-mastered,
the self is the cruelest foe.

When a man has mastered himself,
he is perfectly at ease in cold,
in heat, in pleasure or pain,
in honor or in disgrace.

The mature man, fulfilled in wisdom,
resolute, looks with equal
detachment at a lump of dirt,
a rock, or a piece of pure gold.

He looks impartially on all:
those who love him or hate him,
his kinsmen, his enemies, his friends,
the good, and also the wicked.

The man of yoga should practice
concentration, alone,
mastering mind and body,
free of possessions and desires.

Sitting down, having chosen
a spot that is neither too high
nor too low, that is clean and covered
with a grass mat, a deerskin, and a cloth,

he should concentrate, with his whole
mind, on a single object;
if he practices in this way,
his mind will soon become pure.

With torso and head held straight,
with posture steady and unmoving,
gazing at the tip of his nose,
not letting his eyes look elsewhere,

he should sit there calm, fearless,
firm in his vow to be chaste,
his whole mind controlled, directed,
focused, absorbed in me.

Constantly mastering his mind,
the man of yoga grows peaceful,
attains supreme liberation,
and vanishes into my bliss.

He who eats too much food
or too little, who is always drowsy
or restless, will never succeed
in the yoga of meditation.

For the man who is moderate in food
and pleasure, moderate in action,
moderate in sleep and waking,
yoga destroys all sorrow.

With a mind grown clear and peaceful,
freed from selfish desires,
absorbed in the Self alone,
he is called a true man of yoga.

"A lamp sheltered from the wind
which does not flicker"—to this
is compared the true man of yoga
whose mind has vanished in the Self.

When his mind has become serene
by the practice of meditation,
he sees the Self through the self
and rests in the Self, rejoicing.

He knows the infinite joy
that is reached by the understanding
beyond the senses; steadfast,
he does not fall back from the truth.

Attaining this state, he knows
that there is no higher attainment;
he is rooted there, unshaken
even by the deepest sorrow.

This is true yoga: the unbinding
of the bonds of sorrow. Practice
this yoga with determination
and with a courageous heart.

Abandoning all desires
born of his own selfish will,
a man should learn to restrain
his unruly senses with his mind.

Gradually he becomes calm
and controls his understanding;
focusing on the Self,
he should think of nothing at all.

However often the restless
mind may break loose and wander,
he should rein it in and constantly
bring it back to the Self.

When his mind becomes clear and peaceful,
he enters absolute joy;
his passions are calmed forever;
he is utterly absorbed in God.

Mastering mind and body,
purified from all sin,
he easily gains true freedom
and finds an infinite joy.

Mature in yoga, impartial
everywhere that he looks,
he sees himself in all beings
and all beings in himself.

The man who sees me in everything
and everything within me
will not be lost to me, nor
will I ever be lost to him.

He who is rooted in oneness
realizes that I am
in every being; wherever
he goes, he remains in me.

When he sees all beings as equal
in suffering or in joy
because they are like himself,
that man has grown perfect in yoga.

ARJUNA SAID:

You have taught that the essence of yoga
is equanimity, Krishna;
but since the mind is so restless,
how can that be achieved?

The mind is restless, unsteady,
turbulent, wild, stubborn;
truly, it seems to me
as hard to master as the wind.

THE BLESSED LORD SAID:

You are right, Arjuna: the mind
is restless and hard to master;
but by constant practice and detachment
it *can* be mastered in the end.

Yoga is indeed hard
for those who lack self-restraint;
but if you keep striving earnestly,
in the right way, you can reach it.

ARJUNA SAID:

Krishna, what happens to the man
who, with faith but no self-control,
wanders from the path of yoga
before he becomes mature?

Hasn't he lost both the here
and the hereafter? Doesn't he,
rootless and insubstantial,
fade like a cloud in the sky?

This is the doubt that troubles me,
Krishna; I beg you, please
help me; for only you
can remove this doubt from my mind.

THE BLESSED LORD SAID:

Neither here nor hereafter,
Arjuna, is that man lost;
no one who does good work
will come to an evil end.

Reaching the heaven of the righteous,
after uncountable years
that man will be born again
to parents who are upright and wealthy.

He may even be born to parents
who have practiced yoga and are wise,
though a birth as fortunate as this
is more difficult to obtain.

There he regains the knowledge
acquired in his former life;
and from that point on, Arjuna,
he strives toward the ultimate goal.

Unconsciously he returns
to his former practice; even
a man who asks about yoga
goes beyond formal religion.

Striving, with constant effort,
cleansing himself of all sin
through many lifetimes, at last
he attains the ultimate goal.

The man of yoga is greater
than ascetics, or the learned, or those
who perform the rituals; therefore
be a man of yoga, my son.

Practice yoga sincerely,
with singleminded devotion;
love me with perfect faith;
bring your whole self to me.

Chapter 7

WISDOM AND

REALIZATION

THE BLESSED LORD SAID:

Listen, Arjuna: I will tell you
how you can know me beyond doubt
by practicing nonattachment
and surrendering yourself to me.

I will teach you the essence of this wisdom
and its realization; when you come
to master this, there is nothing
further that needs to be known.

Of ten thousand men, perhaps
one man strives for perfection;
of ten thousand who strive, perhaps
one man knows me in truth.

Earth, fire, water, and wind,
air, mind, and understanding,
and the I-sense: these are the eight
aspects of my physical nature.

This is my lower nature;
but beyond this, I have another,
higher nature; the life
that sustains all beings in the world.

Know that it is the womb
from which all beings arise;
the universe is born within me,
and within me will be destroyed.

There is nothing more fundamental
than I, Arjuna; all worlds,
all beings, are strung upon me
like pearls on a single thread.

I am the taste in water,
the light in the moon and sun,
the sacred syllable *Ôm*
in the Vedas, the sound in air.

I am the fragrance in the earth,
the manliness in men, the brilliance
in fire, the life in the living,
and the abstinence in ascetics.

I am the primal seed
within all beings, Arjuna:
the wisdom of those who know,
the splendor of the high and mighty.

I am the strength of the strong man
who is free of desire and attachment;
I am desire itself
when desire is consistent with duty.

All states of being, whether
marked by *sattva* or *rajas*
or *tamas*, proceed from me;
they are *in* me, not I in them.

Because most men are deluded
by the states of being, they cannot
recognize me, who am
above these, supreme, eternal.

But those men who turn to me
can penetrate beyond this wondrous
power of mine, this magic
created by the three *gunas*.

Others are deluded by my power;
they do not attempt to find me
and, in their ignorance, sink
into demonic evil.

There are four kinds of virtuous men
who worship me, Arjuna: the man
in distress, the man who seeks power,
the man who seeks wisdom, and the sage.

Of these four, the sage is the most
praiseworthy; unattached, steadfast,
that man is supremely beloved
by me, as I am by him.

All these are noble-minded,
but the sage is my very self;
calm, untroubled, he dwells
in the ultimate goal: in me.

At the end of his many lives,
the sage unites with me, thinking,
"Krishna is all that is."
Great souls like this are rare.

Men whose wisdom is darkened
by desires, men who are hemmed in
by the limits of their own natures,
take refuge in other gods.

But whatever the form of reverence,
whatever god a sincere
devotee chooses to worship,
I grant him an unswerving faith.

Empowered by his faith, that man
earnestly seeks the god's favor
and obtains the things he desires,
because I myself have ordained it.

But fleeting is the reward
that men of small minds are given;
they will go to the gods they worship,
but my worshipers come to me.

Though I am unmanifest, fools
think that I have a form,
unaware of my higher existence,
which is permanent and supreme.

Veiled in my mystery and power,
I am not perceived by most men;
their deluded minds cannot see me,
the Unborn, the Changeless, the Undying.

I know all beings who have passed,
and all who live now, Arjuna,
and all who are yet to be;
but I am beyond all knowing.

All beings are born to ignorance,
ruled by aversion and craving;
this, Arjuna, is the primal
duality that keeps them bound.

But when a man is released
from dualities, he can act
purely, without attachment,
and can serve me with all his heart.

Those who take refuge in me,
striving for release from old age
and death, know absolute freedom,
and the Self, and the nature of action.

Those who know me, and the nature
of beings, of gods, and of worship,
are always with me in spirit,
even at the hour of their death.

Chapter 8

ABSOLUTE FREEDOM

ARJUNA SAID:

What is this absolute freedom,
Krishna? What is the Self?
What is the true nature of action,
the nature of beings and of gods?

Teach me the way of worship:
what it is, here, in the body.
And how at the hour of death
can a man be with you in spirit?

THE BLESSED LORD SAID:

Freedom is union with the deathless;
the Self is the essence of all things;
its creative power, called action,
causes the whole world to be.

About beings, know that they die;
about gods, know the Supreme
Person; and know that true worship
is I myself, here, in this body.

Whoever in his final moments
thinks of me only, is sure
to enter my state of being
once his body is dead.

Whatever the state of being
that a man may focus upon
at the end, when he leaves his body,
to that state of being he will go.

Therefore, Arjuna, meditate
on me at all times, and fight;
with your whole mind intent on me,
you will come to me—never doubt it.

Strong in the practice of yoga,
with a mind that is rooted in me
and in nothing else, you will reach
the Supreme Person that I am.

Meditate on the Guide,
the Giver of all, the Primordial
Poet, smaller than an atom,
unthinkable, brilliant as the sun.

If you do this at the hour of your death,
with an unmoving mind, drawing
your breath up between your eyebrows,
you will reach the Person that I am.

I will teach you about the state
called the eternal, the absolute,
which those who strive toward me enter
desireless, freed from attachments.

Closing the nine gates of the body,
keeping the attention in the heart,
drawing the breath to the forehead,
with the mind absorbed, one-pointed,

uttering the sacred *Ôm*,
which itself is freedom, focused
on me as you leave the body,
you attain the ultimate goal.

For men whose minds are forever
focused on me, whose love
has grown deep through meditation,
I am easy to reach, Arjuna.

Reaching me, these great souls
attain the supreme perfection
and no longer are reborn in this fleeting
world of sorrow and pain.

All realms, up to the realm
of Brahma, are subject to rebirth;
but those who attain me, Arjuna,
will never be reborn again.

If you know that one single day
or one single night of Brahma
lasts more than four billion years,
you understand day and night.

When day comes, all things emerge
from the depths of unmanifest nature;
when night comes, all things dissolve
into the unmanifest again.

These multitudes of beings, in an endless,
beginningless cycle, helplessly
dissolve when Brahma's night comes
and emerge once more at his dawn.

But beyond this unmanifest nature
is another unmanifest state,
a primal existence that is not
destroyed when all things dissolve.

This is the eternal unmanifest
and is called the ultimate goal;
men who reach this, my supreme
dwelling, are never reborn.

This Supreme Person, Arjuna,
who contains all beings and extends
to the limits of all that is,
can be reached by wholehearted devotion.

Now, Arjuna, I will tell you
the times at which men of yoga
die and must be reborn,
or die never to return.

Fire, light, day, the moon's brightness,
the six months of the north-turning sun:
dying then, men who are free
go to absolute freedom.

Smoke, gloom, night, the moon's darkness,
the six months of the south-turning sun:
dying then, men of yoga
reach the moon's light and return.

These paths, of light and of darkness,
have always existed; by one,
a man will escape from rebirth;
by the other, he is born again.

Knowing these two paths, Arjuna,
the man of yoga, at all times
resolute in his nonattachment,
goes far beyond the merit

gained from the study of the scriptures,
from acts of worship or control
or charity; dying, he reaches
the supreme, primordial place.

Chapter 9

THE SECRET OF LIFE

THE BLESSED LORD SAID:

Because you trust me, Arjuna,
I will tell you what wisdom is,
the secret of life: know it
and be free of suffering, forever.

This is the supreme wisdom,
the knowing beyond all knowing,
experienced directly, in a flash,
eternal, and a joy to practice.

Those who are without faith
in my teaching, cannot attain me;
they endlessly return to this world,
shuttling from death to death.

I permeate all the universe
in my unmanifest form.
All beings exist within me,
yet I am so inconceivably

vast, so beyond existence,
that though they are brought forth
and sustained by my limitless power,
I am not confined within them.

Just as the all-moving wind,
wherever it goes, always
remains in the vastness of space,
all beings remain within me.

They are gathered back into my womb
at the end of the cosmic cycle—
a hundred fifty thousand
billion of your earthly years—

and as a new cycle begins
I send them forth once again,
pouring from my abundance
the myriad forms of life.

These actions do not bind me, Arjuna.
I stand apart from them all,
indifferent to their outcome,
unattached, serene.

Under my guidance, Nature
brings forth all beings, all things
animate or inanimate,
and sets the whole universe in motion.

Foolish people despise me
in the human form that I take,
blind to my true nature
as the Lord of all life and death.

Their hopes and actions are vain,
their knowledge is sheer delusion;
turning from the light, they fall
into cruelty, selfishness, greed.

But the truly wise, Arjuna,
who dive deep into themselves,
fearless, one-pointed, know me
as the inexhaustible source.

Always chanting my praise,
steadfast in their devotion,
they make their lives an unending
hymn to my endless love.

Others, on the path of knowledge,
know me as the many, the One;
behind the faces of a million
gods, they can see my face.

I am the ritual and the worship,
the medicine and the mantra,
the butter burnt in the fire,
and I am the flames that consume it.

I am the father of the universe
and its mother, essence and goal
of all knowledge, the refiner, the sacred
Ôm, and the threefold Vedas.

I am the beginning and the end,
origin and dissolution,
refuge, home, true lover,
womb and imperishable seed.

I am the heat of the sun,
I hold back the rain and release it;
I am death, and the deathless,
and all that is or is not.

The righteous who follow the scriptures
strictly, who drink the *soma*
and are purified of their sins,
who pray to be taken to heaven —

they reach the world of the gods
and enjoy an indescribable
bliss, although after eons
of those vast and glorious pleasures,

when their merit is spent, they fall back
into the mortal world;
impelled by desire, they achieve
only what will pass away.

But to those who meditate on me
undistracted, and worship me
everywhere, always, I will bring
a reward that never can be lost.

Arjuna, all those who worship
other gods, with deep faith,
are really worshiping me,
even if they don't know it.

For I am the only object
and the only enjoyer of worship;
and they fall back because they cannot
know me as I truly am.

Worshiping the gods, men go
to the gods; worshiping spirits,
to the spirits; worshiping me,
they come to me in the end.

Any offering—a leaf,
a flower or fruit, a cup
of water—I will accept it
if given with a loving heart.

Whatever you do, Arjuna,
do it as an offering to me—
whatever you say or eat
or pray or enjoy or suffer.

In this way you will be freed
from all the results of your actions,
good or harmful; unfettered,
untroubled, you will come to me.

I am the same to all beings;
I favor none and reject none.
But those who worship me live
within me and I live in them.

Even the heartless criminal,
if he loves me with all his heart,
will certainly grow into sainthood
as he moves toward me on this path.

Quickly that man becomes pure,
his heart finds eternal peace.
Arjuna, no one who truly
loves me will ever be lost.

All those who love and trust me,
even the lowest of the low —
prostitutes, beggars, slaves —
will attain the ultimate goal.

How much easier then for ordinary
people, or for those with pure hearts.
In this sad, vanishing world
turn to me and find freedom.

Concentrate your mind on me,
fill your heart with my presence,
love me, serve me, worship me,
and you will attain me at last.

Chapter 10

DIVINE MANIFESTATIONS

THE BLESSED LORD SAID:

Listen further, Arjuna,
to these words that delight your heart;
this is my utmost teaching,
which I tell you for your greatest good.

Neither the myriad gods
nor any of the sages know
my origin; I am the source
from which gods and sages emerge.

Whoever knows me as the Unborn,
the Beginningless, the great Lord
of all worlds—he alone sees
truly and is freed from all harm.

Understanding and wisdom,

patience, truth, peace of mind,

pleasure and pain, being

and nonbeing, fear and courage,

nonviolence, equanimity,

control, benevolence, fame,

dishonor—all these conditions

come forth from me alone.

The seven primeval sages,

the four progenitors from whom

all human beings descend

arose from my own depths, mind-born.

He who can understand

the glory of my manifestations

is forever united with me

by his unwavering love.

I am the source of all things,

and all things emerge from me;

knowing this, wise men worship

by entering my state of being.

Thinking and speaking of me,

enlightening one another,

their lives surrendered to my care,

they are always serene and joyous.

To those who are steadfast, who love me

with true devotion, I give

the yoga of understanding,

which will bring them to where I am.

Acting with deep compassion

from within my own being, I dispel

all ignorance-born darkness

with wisdom's resplendent light.

ARJUNA SAID:

You, Lord, are the supreme

freedom, the supreme abode,

the eternal Person, the primordial

god, all-pervading, birthless.

This is how the great sages
describe you—the divine Narada,
Asita, Devala, and Vyasa—
and now you yourself confirm it.

Everything you have told me,
Krishna, I believe is true;
neither the gods nor the demons
can grasp your infinite forms.

You alone know yourself
through yourself, Lord of all beings,
cause and origin, master
of the universe, God of gods.

Tell me now, in detail,
the divine self-manifestations
by which you pervade these worlds
and grace them with so much splendor.

How can I know you, Krishna?
Which of your many forms
should I visualize, Lord of Yoga,
as I focus my thoughts on you?

Give me some further examples
of your glorious manifestations;
for I never can tire of hearing
your life-giving, honey-sweet words.

THE BLESSED LORD SAID:

All right, Arjuna: I will tell you
a few of my manifestations,
the most glorious ones; for infinite
are the forms in which I appear.

I am the Self, Arjuna,
seated in the heart of all beings;
I am the beginning and the life span
of beings, and their end as well.

Of the sky gods, I am Vishnu;
of the heavenly lights, the sun;
Marichi, chief of the wind gods;
among stars, I am the moon;

of the Vedas, I am the hymns;
Indra among the gods;
the mind among the six senses;
the consciousness of all beings;

of the storm gods, I am Shiva;
of the demigods, Kubera;
Agni among the bright gods;
and Meru, highest of mountains.

Know, Arjuna, that among
priests I am Brihaspati;
of generals, the war god Skanda;
of waters, I am the ocean;

of the great seers, I am Bhrigu;
of words, the syllable *Ôm;*
of worship, I am the mantra;
of mountain chains, Himalaya;

of trees, the sacred fig tree;
of divine sages, Narada;
of the high celestial musicians,
Chitraratha; of saints,

the wise Kapila; of horses,
Ucchaishravas, Indra's
favorite, born of the sea foam;
of elephants, Indra's winged

Airavata; of men,
I am the king; of weapons,
Indra's thunderbolt; of cows,
Kamadhuk, the wish-granter;

Kandarpa, the god of love;
the king of reptiles, Vasuki;
of divine snakes, I am Ananta,
the cosmic serpent; Varuna

among the gods of the ocean;
of the blessed forefathers, I am
Aryaman; of the controllers,
Yama, the god of death;

of demons, the devout Prahlada;
of things that compel, I am time;
the king of animals, the lion;
Garuda among the birds;

of purifiers, the wind;

of warriors, I am Rama;

of sea monsters, Makara;

of rivers, the holy Ganges;

of creations, the beginning and end

and the middle as well, Arjuna;

of knowledge, knowledge of the Self;

of orators, I am the speech;

of letters, the first one, A;

I am imperishable time;

the Creator whose face is everywhere;

death that devours all things;

the source of all things to come;

of feminine powers, I am

fame, wealth, speech, and memory,

intelligence, loyalty, forgiveness;

of chants, I am the great Brihat;

of poetic meters, the *gayatri;*

of months, Margashirsha, the first month;

of seasons, flower-lush spring;

of swindles, I am the dice game;
the splendor of the high and mighty;
determination and victory;
the courage of all brave men;

of the Vrishi clan, I am Krishna;
of Pandavas, I am Arjuna;
of the sages, I am Vyasa;
of poets, the sublime Ushanas;

of punishers, I am the scepter;
the astuteness of the great leaders;
the silence of secret things;
and I am the wisdom of the wise.

I am the divine seed
within all beings, Arjuna;
nothing, inanimate or animate,
could exist for a moment without me.

These are just a small number
of my infinite manifestations;
were I to tell you more,
there would be no end to the telling.

Whatever in this world is excellent
and glows with intelligence or beauty—
be sure that it has its source
in a fragment of my divine splendor.

But what need is there for all these
details? Just know that I am,
and that I support the whole universe
with a single fragment of myself.

Chapter 11

THE COSMIC VISION

ARJUNA SAID:

Graciously, Lord, you have spoken
about the ultimate secret
revealed when one knows the Self,
and your words have cleared up my confusion.

You have told me in detail
the origin and dissolution
of all things, and have described
your own vast, imperishable Being.

I do not doubt that you are
what you say you are, Lord. And yet
I want to see for myself
the splendor of your ultimate form.

If you think I am strong enough,
worthy enough, to endure it,
grant me now, Lord, a vision
of your vast, imperishable Self.

THE BLESSED LORD SAID:

Look, Arjuna: thousands,
millions of my divine forms,
beings of all kinds and sizes,
of every color and shape.

Look: the sun gods, the gods
of fire, dawn, sky, wind, storm,
wonders that no mortal has ever
beheld. Look! Look, Arjuna!

The whole universe, all things
animate or inanimate,
are gathered here—look!—enfolded
inside my infinite body.

But since you are not able
to see me with mortal eyes,
I will grant you divine sight. Look!
Look! The depths of my power!

After he had spoken these words,
Krishna, the great Lord of Yoga,
revealed to Arjuna his majestic,
transcendent, limitless form.

With innumerable mouths and eyes,
faces too marvelous to stare at,
dazzling ornaments, innumerable
weapons uplifted, flaming—

crowned with fire, wrapped
in pure light, with celestial fragrance,
he stood forth as the infinite
God, composed of all wonders.

If a thousand suns were to rise
and stand in the noon sky, blazing,
such brilliance would be like the fierce
brilliance of that mighty Self.

Arjuna saw the whole universe
enfolded, with its countless billions
of life-forms, gathered together
in the body of the God of gods.

Trembling with awe, his blood chilled,
the hair standing up on his flesh,
he bowed and, joining his palms,
spoke these words to the Lord.

ARJUNA SAID:

I see all gods in your body
and multitudes of beings, Lord,
and Brahma on his lotus throne,
and the seers, and the shining angels.

I see you everywhere, with billions
of arms, eyes, bellies, faces,
without end, middle, or beginning,
your body the whole universe, Lord.

Crowned, bearing mace and discus,
you dazzle my vision, blazing
in the measureless, massive, sun-flame
splendor of your radiant form.

You are the deathless, the utmost
goal of all knowledge, the world's base,
the guardian of the eternal
law, the primordial Person.

I see you beginningless, endless,
infinite in power, with a billion
arms, the sun and moon
your eyeballs, the flames of your mouth

lighting the whole universe with splendor.
You alone fill all space,
and the three worlds shudder when they see
your astounding, terrifying form.

Multitudes of gods approach you,
palms joined in dread and wonder;
multitudes of sages chant to you
hymns of deep adoration.

The storm gods, the gods of light,
of sky, dawn, and wind, the angels,
the saints, the demigods and demons,
all gaze at you in amazement.

Your stupendous form, your billions
of eyes, limbs, bellies, mouths, dreadful
fangs: seeing them the worlds
tremble, and so do I.

As you touch the sky, many-hued,
gape-mouthed, your huge eyes blazing,
my innards tremble, my breath
stops, my bones turn to jelly.

Seeing your billion-fanged mouths
blaze like the fires of doomsday,
I faint, I stagger, I despair.
Have mercy on me, Lord Vishnu!

All Dhritarashtra's men
and all these multitudes of kings—
Bhishma, Drona, Karna,
with all our warriors behind them—

are rushing headlong into
your hideous, gaping, knife-fanged
jaws; I see them with skulls crushed,
their raw flesh stuck to your teeth.

As the rivers in many torrents
rush toward the ocean, all
these warriors are pouring down
into your blazing mouths.

As moths rush into a flame
and are burned in an instant, all
beings plunge down your gullet
and instantly are consumed.

You gulp down all worlds, everywhere
swallowing them in your flames,
and your rays, Lord Vishnu, fill all
the universe with dreadful brilliance.

Who *are* you, in this terrifying form?
Have mercy, Lord; grant me even
a glimmer of understanding
to prop up my staggering mind.

THE BLESSED LORD SAID:

I am death, shatterer of worlds,
annihilating all things.
With or without you, these warriors
in their facing armies will die.

Therefore stand up; win glory;
conquer the enemy; rule.
Already I have struck them down;
you are just my instrument, Arjuna.

Drona, Bhishma, Jayadratha,
Karna, and the other great heroes
have already been killed by me. Fight;
without hesitation kill them.

Having heard Krishna's speech,
Arjuna, his palms joined, shivering
with terror, bowed to the Lord
deeply, and stammered these words.

ARJUNA SAID:

Now I know why the universe
delights and rejoices in you;
terrified, the demons scatter
before you, and the sages bow.

Why should they not bow, eternal
Creator, infinite Lord?
You are both being and nonbeing,
and what is beyond them both,

the primal God, the primordial
Person, the ultimate place
of the universe, the knower and the known,
the presence that fills all things.

You are wind, death, fire, the moon,
the Lord of life, the great ancestor
of all things. A thousand times
I bow in front of you, Lord.

Again and again I bow to you,
from all sides, in every direction.
Majesty infinite in power,
you pervade — no, you *are* — all things.

If, thinking you a human, I ever
touched you or patted your back
or called you "dear fellow" or "friend"
through negligence or affection,

or greeted you with disrespect,
thoughtlessly, when we were playing
or resting, alone or in public,
I beg you to forgive me, immeasurable

God, great father of the world,
teacher, sustainer, goal
of all reverence, unique and peerless
Lord of unthinkable splendor.

Therefore, most sincerely, I beg
your pardon. As a father forgives
his son, a friend his dear friend,
a lover his beloved: forgive me.

Having seen what no mortal has seen,
I am joyful, yet I quiver with dread.
Show me your other form — please —
the one that I know; have mercy;

let me see you as you were before,
crowned, bearing mace and discus,
with only four arms, O billion-armed
Lord of infinite forms.

THE BLESSED LORD SAID:

Graciously for your sake, Arjuna,
I showed you my highest form —
dazzling, infinite, primal —
which no one has seen but you.

Not by worship or study
or alms or ascetic practice
can I be seen in this form
by anyone but you, Arjuna.

Do not be frightened or confused
at seeing my horrific form.
Free of fear, lighthearted,
see me as I was before.

Having spoken thus to Arjuna,
the Lord stood before him again
in the mild and pleasant form
of Krishna, the kind, the beautiful.

ARJUNA SAID:

Seeing your human form,
Krishna, I feel at ease;
once more I am myself,
and my mind has regained its composure.

THE BLESSED LORD SAID:

The vision that you have been granted
is difficult to attain;
even the gods are always
longing to behold me like this.

Not by study or rites
or alms or ascetic practice
can I be seen in this cosmic
form, as you have just seen me.

Only by single-minded
devotion can I be known
as I truly am, Arjuna—
can I be seen and entered.

He who acts for my sake,
loving me, free of attachment,
with benevolence toward all beings,
will come to me in the end.

Chapter 12

THE YOGA OF DEVOTION

ARJUNA SAID:

One man loves you with pure
devotion; another man loves
the Unmanifest. Which of these two
understands yoga more deeply?

THE BLESSED LORD SAID:

Those who love and revere me
with unwavering faith, always
centering their minds on me —
they are the most perfect in yoga.

But those who revere the Imperishable,
the Unsayable, the Unmanifest,
the All-Present, the Inconceivable,
the Exalted, the Unchanging, the Eternal,

mastering their senses, acting
at all times with equanimity,
rejoicing in the welfare of all beings—
they too will reach me at last.

But *their* path is much more arduous
because, for embodied beings,
the Unmanifest is obscure,
and difficult to attain.

Those who love and revere me,
who surrender all actions to me,
who meditate upon me
with undistracted attention,

whose minds have entered my being—
I come to them all, Arjuna,
and quickly rescue them all
from the ocean of death and birth.

Concentrate every thought
on me alone; with a mind
fully absorbed, one-pointed,
you will live within me, forever.

If you find that you are unable
to center your thoughts on me,
strengthen your mind by the steady
practice of concentration.

If this is beyond your powers,
dedicate yourself to me;
performing all actions for my sake,
you will surely achieve success.

If even this is beyond you,
rely on my basic teaching:
act always without attachment,
surrendering your action's fruits.

Knowledge is better than practice;
meditation is better
than knowledge; and best of all
is surrender, which soon brings peace.

He who has let go of hatred,
who treats all beings with kindness
and compassion, who is always serene,
unmoved by pain or pleasure,

free of the "I" and "mine,"
self-controlled, firm and patient,
his whole mind focused on me —
that man is the one I love best.

He who neither disturbs
the world nor is disturbed by it,
who is free of all joy, fear, envy —
that man is the one I love best.

He who is pure, impartial,
skilled, unworried, calm,
selfless in all undertakings —
that man is the one I love best.

He who, devoted to me,
is beyond joy and hatred, grief
and desire, good and bad fortune —
that man is the one I love best.

The same to both friend and foe,
the same in disgrace or honor,
suffering or joy, untroubled,
indifferent to praise and blame,

quiet, filled with devotion,
content with whatever happens,
at home wherever he is—
that man is the one I love best.

Those who realize the essence
of duty, who trust me completely
and surrender their lives to me—
I love them with very great love.

Chapter 13

THE FIELD AND
ITS KNOWER

ARJUNA SAID:

What are Nature and Self?
What are the field and its Knower,
knowledge and the object of knowledge?
Teach me about them, Krishna.

THE BLESSED LORD SAID:

This body is called the field,
Arjuna; the one who watches
whatever happens within it—
wise men call him the Knower.

I am the Knower of the field
in every body, Arjuna;
genuine knowledge means knowing
both the field and its Knower.

Listen, and I will explain
the nature of the field, what changes
take place in it, who is the Knower,
and what his great powers are.

The sages have sung of these truths
in the sacred hymns and in many
powerful and well-argued
reasonings about God.

The five elements, the I-sense,
the understanding, the ten
senses, the mind, the unmanifest,
and the five domains of the senses,

desire and aversion, pleasure
and pain, consciousness, will —
all these components make up
the field, with its various changes.

Humility, patience, sincerity,
nonviolence, uprightness, purity,
devotion to one's spiritual teacher,
constancy, self-control,

dispassion toward objects of the senses,
freedom from the I-sense, insight
into the evils of birth,
sickness, old age, and death,

detachment, absence of clinging
to son, wife, family, and home,
an unshakable equanimity
in good fortune or in bad,

an unwavering devotion to me
above all things, an intense
love of solitude, distaste
for involvement in worldly affairs,

persistence in knowing the Self
and awareness of the goal of knowing—
all this is called true knowledge;
what differs from it is called ignorance.

I will teach you what should be known;
knowing it, you are immortal;
it is the supreme reality,
which transcends both being and nonbeing.

Its hands and its feet are everywhere;
everywhere its eyes, heads, mouths,
everywhere its ears; it dwells
in all worlds, containing all things.

Though lacking senses itself,
it shines through the working of the senses;
unattached, all-sustaining,
experiencing the *gunas* yet above them,

outside yet within all beings,
motionless, always moving,
subtle beyond comprehension,
far yet nearer than near,

indivisible, though it seems
divided in separate bodies,
it is what sustains all things,
what devours them, what creates them.

It is the light of lights,

beyond all darkness; it is knowledge,

the object and goal of all knowledge;

it is seated in the hearts of all beings.

This, in brief, is the field,

knowledge, and the object of knowledge;

a devotee who understands this

is ready for my state of being.

Know that both Nature and Self

are equally without beginning,

and know that Nature gives rise

to changes in the field and to *gunas*.

Nature is the cause of any

activity in the body;

the Self is the cause of any

feelings of pleasure or pain.

The Self, abiding in Nature,

experiences the *gunas;* its attachment

to the *gunas* causes its birth

in good wombs or evil wombs.

It is called the witness, the consenter,
the sustainer, the enjoyer, the great Lord,
and also the highest Self,
the supreme Person in this body.

He who thus knows the Self
as separate from Nature and the *gunas*
will never be born again,
whatever path he may follow.

By meditation, some men
can see the Self in the self;
others, by the yoga of knowledge;
others, by selfless action.

Still others, not seeing, only
hear about it and worship;
they too cross beyond death,
trusting in what they have heard.

Whatever exists, Arjuna,
animate or inanimate,
has come into existence
from the union of field and Knower.

He who sees that the great Lord
is equally in all beings,
deathless when every being
dies—that man sees truly.

Seeing the great Lord everywhere,
he knows beyond doubt that he cannot
harm the Self by the self,
and he reaches the highest goal.

He who sees that all actions
are performed by Nature alone
and thus that the self is not
the doer—that man sees truly.

When he sees that the myriad beings
emanate from the One
and have their source in the One,
that man gains absolute freedom.

This supreme Self is beginningless,
deathless, and unconfined;
although it inhabits bodies,
it neither acts nor is tainted.

Just as all-present space
is too rarified to be tainted,
so the Self is untainted
by dwelling within a body.

Just as the sun by itself
illumines the entire world,
so the field owner illumines
everything in the field.

He whose inner eye sees
how the Knower is distinct from the field,
and how men are set free from Nature,
arrives at the highest state.

Chapter 14

THE THREE *GUNAS*

THE BLESSED LORD SAID:

I will teach you further about true
knowledge, ultimate knowledge,
which all the sages have mastered
and gone to supreme perfection.

Relying on this, and attaining
a state like mine, they neither
are reborn when the world is created
nor grieve when it is dissolved.

Nature, for me, is a womb;
in Nature I plant my seed,
and from this seed of mine bursts forth
the origin of all beings.

Whatever life-forms, Arjuna,
develop in any womb,
Nature is their primal womb
and I am their seed-giving father.

The three *gunas*, born of Nature—
sattva, rajas, and *tamas*—
bind to the mortal body
the deathless embodied Self.

Of these three, *sattva*, untainted,
luminous, free from sorrow,
binds by means of attachment
to knowledge and joy, Arjuna.

Rajas is marked by passion
born of craving and attachment;
it binds the embodied Self
to never-ending activity.

Tamas, ignorance-born,
deludes all embodied beings;
it binds them, Arjuna, by means of
dullness, indolence, and sleep.

Sattva causes attachment
to joy, *rajas* to action,
and *tamas,* obscuring knowledge,
attaches beings to dullness.

Sattva prevails when it masters
rajas and *tamas* both;
rajas or *tamas* prevails
when it masters the other two.

When the light of knowledge shines forth
through all the gates of the body,
then it is apparent
that *sattva* is the ruling trait.

Greed and constant activity,
excessive projects, cravings,
restlessness: these arise
when *rajas* is the ruling trait.

Darkness, dullness, stagnation,
indolence, confusion, torpor,
inertia: these appear
when *tamas* is the ruling trait.

If a being dies in a state
where the quality of *sattva* prevails,
he goes to the stainless heavens
of those who have seen the truth.

If he dies when *rajas* prevails,
he is born among those attached
to action; if *tamas* prevails,
he is born among the deluded.

The fruit of action well done
is *sattvic* and without a stain;
but the fruit of *rajas* is suffering,
and ignorance the fruit of *tamas*.

From *sattva*, knowledge is born;
from *rajas*, restlessness and greed;
dullness and confusion arise
from *tamas*, and ignorance also.

Men of *sattva* go upward;
men of *rajas* remain
in between; men of *tamas*,
lowest of all, sink downward.

When a man sees clearly that there is
no doer besides the *gunas*
and knows what exists beyond them,
he can enter my state of being.

Going beyond the three *gunas*
that arise from the body, freed
from the sorrows of birth, old age,
and death, he attains the Immortal.

ARJUNA SAID:

How can I recognize the man
who has gone beyond the three *gunas?*
What has he done to go
beyond them? How does he act?

THE BLESSED LORD SAID:

Whatever quality arises —
light, activity, delusion —
he neither dislikes its presence
nor desires it when it is not there.

He who is unattached,
who is not disturbed by the *gunas*,
who is firmly rooted and knows
that only the *gunas* are acting,

who is equally self-contained
in pain or pleasure, in happiness
or sorrow, who is content
with whatever happens, who sees

dirt, rocks, and gold as equal,
who is unperturbed amid praise
or blame of himself, indifferent
to honor and to disgrace,

serene in success and failure,
impartial to friend and foe,
unattached to action — that man
has gone beyond the three *gunas*.

He who faithfully serves me
with the yoga of devotion, going
beyond the three *gunas*, is ready
to attain the ultimate freedom.

For I am the foundation
of that birthless, imperishable freedom,
the basis of eternal duty
and of limitless, perfect joy.

Chapter 15

THE ULTIMATE PERSON

THE BLESSED LORD SAID:

This realm of sorrow is the world tree
that the sages describe: its roots
above, its branches below,
its green leaves the sacred hymns.

Its branches, spreading below
and above, are fed by the *gunas*,
and bud into objects of the senses;
its roots, causing action, stretch down

into the world of men;
men here on earth cannot see
how vast and extensive its form is
or where it begins and ends.

Cut down this deep-rooted tree
with the sharp-edged ax of detachment;
then search for that primal Person
from whom the whole universe flows.

Find him in the place that one enters
and does not return from; without
arrogance or delusion,
intent on the Self alone,

serene, with desires extinguished,
released from pleasure and pain,
from joy and suffering, the wise
attain that eternal state.

The sun does not give it light,
nor the moon, nor does any fire;
those who reach it, my highest
dwelling, are never reborn.

One fragment of me, becoming
an eternal soul in the world,
draws to itself the mind
and the other five Nature-born senses.

When the Lord takes on a body
or leaves it, he carries these senses
just as the wind carries fragrances
from the places where it has been.

Presiding over the senses
of hearing and sight, of touch,
taste, smell, and also of mind,
he savors the senses' objects.

Whether he leaves or remains,
enjoying his contact with the *gunas*,
the deluded see nothing; but wise men
see him with their inner eye.

True men of yoga, striving,
see him within themselves;
but men without self-control,
however they strive, do not see him.

The brilliance of the moon, of fire,
the brilliance that flames from the sun
to illumine the entire world —
this brilliance in truth is mine.

Entering the earth, I support
all beings by my life-giving power;
becoming the nectar-filled moonlight,
I cause plants and herbs to thrive.

I am the vital fire
in the bellies of all men; joined
with the breath as it flows, I digest
the various kinds of food.

I dwell deep in the hearts
of all beings; I am the source
of memory and knowledge, the author
of all scriptures, their wisdom, their goal.

In this world, there are two persons:
the transient and the eternal,
all beings are transient as bodies,
but eternal within the Self.

Yet beyond these two is the ultimate
Person, the highest Self,
the immutable Lord who, entering
the universe, brings it to life.

I am beyond the transient
and am higher than the eternal;
therefore, scriptures and world
call me the Ultimate Person.

Whoever, clear-minded, knows me
as the Ultimate Person, knows
all that is truly worth knowing,
and he loves me with all his heart.

Thus, Arjuna, I have taught you
this most secret doctrine; whoever
learns it, is wise, and has done
all that there is to do.

Chapter 16

DIVINE TRAITS AND DEMONIC TRAITS

THE BLESSED LORD SAID:

Fearlessness, purity of heart,
persistence in the yoga of knowledge,
generosity, self-control,
nonviolence, gentleness, candor,

integrity, disengagement,
joy in the study of the scriptures,
compassion for all beings, modesty,
patience, a tranquil mind,

dignity, kindness, courage,
a benevolent, loving heart —
these are the qualities of men
born with divine traits, Arjuna.

Hypocrisy, insolence, anger,
cruelty, ignorance, conceit —
these, Arjuna, are the qualities
of men with demonic traits.

The divine traits lead to freedom;
the demonic, to suffering and bondage.
But do not be concerned, Arjuna:
the traits you have are divine.

The demonic and the divine
are the two kinds of men in this world.
The divine I have told you about;
now learn about the demonic.

Demonic men do not realize
what should and what should not be done;
there is no purity of heart,
no virtue, no truth inside them.

They say that life is an accident
caused by sexual desire,
that the universe has no moral
order, no truth, no God.

Clinging to this stupid belief,
drawn into cruelty and malice,
they become lost souls and, at last,
enemies of the whole world.

Driven by insatiable lusts,
drunk on the arrogance of power,
hypocritical, deluded,
their actions foul with self-seeking,

tormented by a vast anxiety
that continues until their death,
convinced that the gratification
of desire is life's sole aim,

bound by a hundred shackles
of hope, enslaved by their greed,
they squander their time dishonestly
piling up mountains of wealth.

"Today I got this desire,
and tomorrow I will get that one;
all these riches are mine,
and soon I will have even more.

"Already I have killed these enemies,
and soon I will kill the rest;
I am the lord, the enjoyer,
successful, happy, and strong,

"noble, and rich, and famous.
Who on earth is my equal?
I will worship, give alms, and rejoice."
Thus think these ignorant fools.

Bewildered by endless thinking,
entangled in the net of delusion,
addicted to desire, they plunge
into the foulest of hells.

Self-centered, stubborn, filled
with all the insolence of wealth,
they go through the outward forms
of worship, but their hearts are elsewhere.

Clinging to the I-sense, to power,
to arrogance, lust, and rage,
they hate me, denying my presence
in their own and in others' bodies.

Through all the cycles of birth
and death, I hurl these depraved,
cruel, and hate-filled men
into demonic wombs.

Trapped in demonic wombs,
deluded in birth after birth,
they never reach me, Arjuna,
but sink to the lowest state.

This is the soul-destroying
threefold entrance to hell:
desire, anger, and greed.
Every man should avoid them.

The man who refuses to enter
these three gates into darkness
does what is best for himself
and attains the ultimate goal.

But the man who rejects the scriptures,

chasing his own desires,

cannot attain the goal

of true joy or true success.

Therefore, guided by the scriptures,

know what to do and not do;

first understand their injunctions,

then act uprightly in the world.

Chapter 17

THREE KINDS OF FAITH

ARJUNA SAID:

There are men who worship with faith,
and yet who reject the scriptures.
What *guna* prevails in them, Lord?
Sattva, rajas, or *tamas?*

THE BLESSED LORD SAID:

There are three kinds of faith in men,
each kind ruled by the *guna*
inherent in the nature of the man.
Listen as I explain this.

Every man's faith conforms
with his inborn nature, Arjuna.
Faith is a person's core;
whatever his faith is, *he* is.

Sattvic men worship the gods;
rajasic, demigods and demons;
tamasic, the hordes of dark
spirits and the ghosts of the dead.

Men who mortify their flesh
in ways not sanctioned by the scriptures,
who are trapped in their sense of "I"
and driven by warped desires,

in their folly torturing the parts
that compose the body, and thus
torturing *me* in the body—
know that their aim is demonic.

There are three kinds of food as well;
and worship, control, and charity
also divide into three kinds.
Here are the distinctions among them:

Foods that the *sattvic* are drawn to
promote vitality, health,
pleasure, strength, and long life,
and are fresh, firm, succulent, and tasty.

Foods that please the *rajasic*—
bitter or salty or sour,
hot or harsh or pungent—
cause pain, disease, and discomfort.

The preferred foods of the *tamasic*
are stale, overcooked, tasteless,
contaminated, impure,
filthy, putrid, and rotten.

Worship that is offered according
to scripture, for the sake of the worship,
without any thought of reward—
this kind of worship is *sattvic*.

Rajasic worship, Arjuna,
is offered out of desire,
for the good that it will result in
or in order to gain respect.

Worship is *tamasic* when
it is faithless, contrary to scripture,
with no food offered, no texts
recited, no payment to the priest.

Honoring the gods, the priests,
the teachers and sages, purity,
nonviolence, chastity, uprightness—
all this is control of the body.

Speaking the truth with kindness,
honesty that causes no pain,
and the recitation of scripture—
this is control of speech.

Serenity, gentleness, silence,
benevolence, self-restraint,
purity of being, compassion—
this is control of the mind.

When these three levels of control
are practiced with faith and diligence
and with no desire for results,
such control is called *sattvic.*

Rajasic control—by its nature
wavering and unstable—
is performed out of pride or to gain
respect, admiration, and honor.

Control is called *tamasic*
when used by deluded men
to mortify their flesh or to gain
the power to cause harm to others.

Charity given to the worthy,
without any expectations,
for the sake of the act itself—
this kind of charity is *sattvic*.

Rajasic charity is given
halfheartedly, with the thought
of securing some favor in return
or to gain some spiritual merit.

Charity is called *tamasic*
when given to the undeserving,
at the wrong time and wrong place,
grudgingly, without respect.

Ôm Tat Sat: these words
stand for the liberated mind
by which priests, scriptures, and rituals
were appointed in ancient times.

Therefore, the word Ôm is always
chanted, by those who expound
the scriptures, to begin an act
of worship, control, or charity.

Tat—which means "That," "the Absolute"—
is chanted by seekers of freedom
whenever they perform right actions
with no concern for results.

The third word, Sat, has the sense
of "reality," "goodness"; thus
Sat is used to denote
any praiseworthy action.

Maturity of worship or control
or charity is also called Sat,
as is all unselfish action
that leads to any of the three.

But worship, control, or charity
offered without faith, Arjuna,
is called *Asat,* "unreal,"
and is worthless, in this world or the next.

Chapter 18

FREEDOM THROUGH RENUNCIATION

ARJUNA SAID:

Teach me this lesson, Krishna:
what it means to renounce,
what it means to relinquish,
and the difference between the two.

THE BLESSED LORD SAID:

To give up desire-bound actions
is what is meant by *renouncing;*
to give up the results of all actions
is what the wise call *to relinquish.*

Some sages say that all action
is tainted and should be relinquished;
others permit only acts
of worship, control, and charity.

Here is the truth: these acts
of worship, control, and charity
purify the heart and therefore
should not be relinquished but performed.

But even the most praiseworthy acts
should be done with complete nonattachment
and with no concern for results;
this is my final judgment.

Relinquishment is of three kinds:
When any obligatory action
is relinquished because of delusive
thinking — that is *tamasic.*

When a man relinquishes action
because it is hard or painful —
that relinquishment is *rajasic,*
and cannot guide him toward freedom.

But when, out of duty, a man
performs an obligatory action,
relinquishing all results —
that relinquishment is called *sattvic.*

The man who is able to relinquish,
beyond doubt, does not avoid
unpleasant actions, nor is he
attached to actions that are pleasant.

An embodied being can never
relinquish actions completely;
to relinquish the *results* of actions
is all that can be required.

For those who cling to it, action
has three results when they die —
desired, undesired, and mixed;
but for those who renounce, it has none.

Now I will teach you the five
elements that must be present
for an action to be accomplished,
as philosophers have declared:

the physical body, the agent,

the various organs of sense,

the various kinds of behavior,

and divine providence as fifth.

In whatever action a man takes

with his body, his speech, or his mind,

whether it is right or wrong,

these five things must be present.

Since this is so, when a man

of limited understanding

sees himself as sole agent,

he is not seeing the truth.

A man who is free from the I-sense

and is pure, even if he kills

these warriors, does not kill,

nor is he bound by his actions.

Knowledge, the known, and the knower

are the three things that motivate action;

instrument, action, and agent

are the three components of action.

Knowledge, action, and agent
are of three kinds, according to the *guna*
that prevails in each one. Listen,
and I will explain these distinctions.

Knowledge that sees in all things
a single, imperishable being,
undivided among the divided —
this kind of knowledge is *sattvic.*

Rajasic knowledge perceives
a multiplicity of beings,
each one existing by itself,
separate from all the others.

Knowledge is called *tamasic*
when it clings to one thing as if it
were the whole, and has no concern
for the true cause and essence of things.

Obligatory action, performed
without any craving or aversion
by a man unattached to results —
this kind of action is *sattvic.*

Rajasic action is performed
with a wish to satisfy desires,
with the thought "I am doing this,"
and with an excessive effort.

Action is *tamasic* when
it begins in delusion, with no
concern that it may cause
harm to oneself or others.

An agent who is free from attachment
and the I-sense, courageous, steadfast,
unmoved by success or failure —
this kind of agent is *sattvic*.

A *rajasic* agent is impulsive,
seeks to obtain results,
is greedy, violent, impure,
and buffeted by joy and sorrow.

An agent is called *tamasic*
when he is undisciplined, stupid,
stubborn, mean, deceitful,
lazy, and easily depressed.

Listen as I describe
the three kinds of understanding
and the three kinds of will, according
to the *guna* that prevails in each.

The understanding that knows
what to do and what not to,
safety and danger, bondage
and liberation, is *sattvic.*

Rajasic understanding
fails to know right from wrong,
when from when not to act,
what should from what should not be done.

Understanding is *tamasic*
when, thickly covered in darkness,
it imagines that wrong is right
and sees the world upside down.

The unswerving will that controls
the functions of mind, breath, senses
by the practice of meditation —
this kind of will is *sattvic.*

Rajasic will is attached
to duty, sensual pleasures,
power, and wealth, with anxiety
and a constant desire for results.

That will is called *tamasic*
by which a stupid man keeps
clinging to grief and fear,
to torpor, depression, and conceit.

Now, Arjuna, I will tell you
about the three kinds of happiness.
The happiness which comes from long practice,
which leads to the end of suffering,

which at first is like poison, but at last
like nectar—this kind of happiness,
arising from the serenity
of one's own mind, is called *sattvic*.

Rajasic happiness comes
from contact between the senses
and their objects, and is at first
like nectar, but at last like poison.

Happiness is called *tamasic*
when it is self-deluding
from beginning to end, and arises
from sleep, indolence, and dullness.

No being on earth, Arjuna,
or among the blithe gods in heaven
is free from the conditioning
of these three Nature-born *gunas*.

The duties of priests, of warriors,
of laborers, and of servants
are apportioned according to the *gunas*
that arise from their inborn nature.

Serenity, control, austerity,
uprightness, purity, patience,
knowledge, piety, and judgment
are the natural duties of priests.

Boldness, the ability to lead,
largeheartedness, courage in battle,
energy, stamina, and strength
are the natural duties of warriors.

Farming, cowherding, and trade
are the natural duties of laborers;
serving the needs of others
is the natural duty of servants.

Content with his natural duty,
each one achieves success.
Listen now: I will tell you
how this success can be found.

A man finds success by worshiping
with his own right actions the One
from whom all actions arise
and by whom the world is pervaded.

It is better to do your own duty
badly than to perfectly do
another's; when you do your duty,
you are naturally free from sin.

No one should relinquish his duty,
even though it is flawed;
all actions are enveloped by flaws
as fire is enveloped by smoke.

Self-mastered, with mind unattached
at all times, beyond desire,
one attains through renunciation
the supreme freedom from action.

Learn from me briefly, Arjuna,
that when a man gains success
he also gains perfect freedom,
the ultimate state of knowledge.

With a purified understanding,
fully mastering himself,
relinquishing all sense-objects,
released from aversion and craving,

solitary, eating lightly,
controlling speech, mind, and body,
absorbed in deep meditation
at all times, calm, impartial,

free from the "I" and "mine,"
from aggression, arrogance, greed,
desire, and anger, he is fit
for the state of absolute freedom.

Serene in this state of freedom,
beyond desire and sorrow,
seeing all beings as equal,
he attains true devotion to me.

By devotion he comes to realize
the meaning of my infinite vastness;
when he knows who I truly am,
he instantly enters my being.

Relying on me in his actions
and performing them for my sake,
he reaches, by my great kindness,
the eternal, unchanging place.

Give up all actions to me;
love me above all others;
steadfastly keep your mind
focused on me alone.

Focused on me at all times,
you will overcome all obstructions;
but if you persist in clinging
to the I-sense, then you are lost.

And even if, clinging to the I-sense,
you say that you will not fight,
your intention will be in vain:
Nature will compel you to act.

The thing that, in your delusion,
you wish not to do, you will do,
even against your will,
since your own karma binds you.

The Lord dwells deep in the heart
of all beings, by his wondrous power
making them all revolve
like puppets on a carousel.

Devoted to him, Arjuna,
take refuge in him alone;
by his kindness, you will attain
the state of imperishable peace.

Thus I have taught you the secret
of secrets, the utmost knowledge;
meditate deeply upon it,
then act as you think best.

Now listen to my final words,
the deepest secret of all;
I am speaking for your own welfare,
since you are precious to me.

If you focus your mind on me
and revere me with all your heart,
you will surely come to me; this
I promise, because I love you.

Relinquishing all your duties,
take refuge in me alone.
Do not fear: I will free you
from the evils of birth and death.

These teachings must not be spoken
to men without self-control
and piety, or to men
whose hearts are closed to my words.

He who teaches this primal
secret to those who love me
has acted with the greatest love
and will come to me, beyond doubt.

No one can do me a service
that is more devoted than this,
and no one on earth is more
precious to me than *he* is.

Whoever earnestly studies
this sacred discourse of ours—
I consider that he has worshiped
and loved me with the yoga of knowledge.

Even the man who hears it
with faith and an open mind—
he also, released, will go to
the joyous heavens of the pure.

Have you truly heard me, Arjuna?
Has my teaching entered your heart?
Have my words now driven away
your ignorance and delusion?

ARJUNA SAID:

Krishna, I see the truth now,
by your immeasurable kindness.
I have no more doubts; I will act
according to your command.

SANJAYA SAID:

O King, as I heard this wondrous
discourse between Lord Krishna
and Arjuna, the man of great soul,
the hair stood up on my flesh.

By the poet Vyasa's kindness,
I heard this most secret doctrine
directly from the mighty Lord
of Yoga, Krishna himself.

O King, the more I remember
this wondrous and holy discourse
between the Lord and Arjuna,
the more I shudder with joy.

And as often as I remember
the Lord's vast, wondrous form,
each time I am astonished;
each time I shudder with joy.

Where Krishna is—Lord of Yoga—
and Arjuna the archer: there,
surely, I think, is splendor
and virtue and spiritual wealth.

Notes to the Introduction

p. 13 *"It was the first of books"* The Journals and Mis-
cellaneous Notebooks of Ralph Waldo Emerson, vol. X,
1847–1848, ed. Merton M. Sealts, Jr., The Belknap Press of
Harvard University Press, 1973, p. 360.

p. 13 *"The reader is nowhere raised"* Henry David
Thoreau, A Week on the Concord and Merrimack Rivers,
Walden, The Maine Woods, Cape Cod, Library of Amer-
ica, 1985, pp. 111, 116. "Geeta" here, like "Kreeshna" and
"Arjoon" in the passage from Thoreau quoted in a later note,
is the spelling used in the first English translation, by
Charles Wilkins, published in 1785.

pp. 13–14 *"stupendous and cosmogonal"* "In the morn-
ing I bathe my intellect in the stupendous and cosmogonal
philosophy of the Bhagvat Geeta, since whose composition
years of the gods have elapsed, and in comparison with which
our modern world and its literature seem puny and trivial" (A
Week on the Concord, p. 559). The Gita was one of the books
that Thoreau took with him on his retreat to Walden Pond.

p. 14 *a Sufi sheikh* Abu Sa'id ibn Abi'l Khayr (967–1049).

Reynold Alleyne Nicholson, *Studies in Islamic Mysticism,* Cambridge University Press, 1921, p. 56.

p. 15   *"wondrous dialogue"*   Gita 18.74.

pp. 15–16 *from beginning to end didactic*   It must be confessed that in its last third the poem often becomes merely a versified philosophical tract, much inferior to its first two-thirds, both poetically and spiritually. Chapter 12, though it has its virtues, has justifiably been called the greatest anticlimax in world literature. In chapters 13 to 18 much of the material is dull and secondary at best; for long stretches the poem seems to be written by a scholastic philosopher bent on categorizing everything in the world according to the three *gunas.*

There is as well a noticeable difference in attitude between the first two-thirds and the last third, on at least three points. The attitudes can be summarized as follows:

THE SCRIPTURES. *Chapters 2–12:* The scriptures dwell in the realm of duality and the three *gunas,* which should be transcended. They are unnecessary for anyone who has directly experienced the truth. (2.45–46, 2.52–53) The righteous, those who follow the scriptures strictly, go to heaven but do not go to Krishna. (9.20–21) *Chapters 13–18:* Let yourself be guided by the scriptures in everything you do; it is important to understand them before you act. (16.24)

THE WICKED. *Chapters 2–12:* Krishna includes everyone in his embrace. Even outcastes and criminals can turn
to him and become saints. (9.29–30) The sage sees himself in all beings and all beings in himself. (6.29) He treats
all beings with equal compassion, even the wicked. (6.9)
Chapters 13–18: People are born with either divine or demonic traits. (16.1ff.) Lifetime after lifetime, Krishna hurls
the wicked into demonic wombs, and they can never reach
him. (16.19–20)

THE SELF. *Chapters 2–12:* Krishna is the Self seated in
the heart of all beings. (10.20) *Chapters 13–18:* Krishna is
the ultimate Self, which is higher than the eternal Self in all
beings. (15.17)

It is clear that these two parts of the Gita have been
written either from different levels of consciousness or to
different kinds of readers. No one knows, of course, how
the Gita was edited or what its original form was. But two
possibilities come to mind. The first is that chapters 13 to
18 are an addition to the Gita, written by a poet who was
less spiritually evolved than the author of the first two-
thirds of the poem. The second possibility is that these later
chapters were written by the same poet, out of compassion
for less mature readers, readers who will never understand
the truth as taught in the earlier part of the Gita, but who
may nevertheless learn to improve themselves within the
limits of conventional worship. If this second possibility is

the correct one, the poet's intention is admirable, however dull this may make some of the later chapters. (The great Zen Master Yang-shan said, "In my shop I handle all kinds of merchandise. If someone comes looking for rat shit, I'll sell him rat shit. If someone comes looking for gold, I'll sell him pure gold.")

Still, it is hard to see how the extremely dualistic and judgmental morality of chapter 16, which makes demons of a considerable portion of the human race, could be helpful to even the most conventional devotee. After all, as Lao-tzu says,

> What is a good man but a bad man's teacher?
> What is a bad man but a good man's job?
> If you don't understand this, you will get lost,
> however intelligent you are.
> It is the great secret.

> (Stephen Mitchell, *Tao Te Ching: A New English Version*, HarperCollins, 1988, chapter 27.)

p. 17 *"The idea that there is a goal"* *Day by Day with Bhagavan*, A. Devaraja Mudaliar, Sri Ramanasramam, 1977, p. 15. Maharshi also said, "Peace is our real nature. We spoil it. What is required is that we stop spoiling it. We are not going to create peace anew. For instance, originally there is nothing but space in a room. We fill it up with various objects. If we want space, all we need do is to remove all those objects, and we get space. In the same way, if we remove all the rubbish, all the thoughts, from our minds, peace will appear. What is obstructing the peace has to be removed. Peace is the only reality." (p. 111)

p. 17 *directly contradictory to the deeper lessons*   See Gandhi's "The Message of the Gita" from *The Collected Works of Mahatma Gandhi*, vol. XLI, The Publications Division, Ministry of Information and Broadcasting, Government of India, 1970, pp. 93–101, reprinted here in the Appendix. Gandhi's essay is the clearest restatement of Krishna's teaching I have found. He is talking about the Gita from the inside, and his devotion to it is palpable. (Elsewhere he says, "The Gita is my eternal mother. Whenever I am in difficulty or distress, I seek refuge in her bosom.") That is what makes his view of its inadequacies so convincing. The Gita is, for him, a sacred text, the most sacred of texts, but not God's final word. What was true for a warrior culture is not necessarily true for us. "What may be permissible at one time, or in one place, may not be so at another time and in another place. Desire for [the] fruit [of action] is the only universal prohibition."

p. 17 *an enlightened sage, who cherishes all beings*

Freed from the endless cycle
of birth and death, they can act

impartially toward all beings,
since to them all beings are the same. (5.19)

The wise man, cleansed of his sins,
who has cut off all separation,
who delights in the welfare of all beings . . . (5.25)

He who acts for my sake,
loving me, free of attachment,
with benevolence toward all beings . . . (11.55)

He who has let go of hatred,
who treats all beings with kindness
and compassion . . .
that man is the one I love best. (12.13−14)

p. 17 *whatever Krishna may say* In spite of Thoreau's reverence for the Gita, he is appropriately resistant on this point: "Kreeshna's argument, it must be allowed, is defective. No sufficient reason is given why Arjoon should fight. Arjoon may be convinced, but the reader is not. . . . What is 'a man's own particular calling'? What are the duties which are appointed by one's birth? It is a defence of the institution of cast[e]s, of what is called the 'natural duty' of the Kshetree, or soldier, 'to attach himself to the discipline,' 'not to flee from the field,' and the like. But they who are unconcerned about the consequences of their actions are not therefore unconcerned about their actions" (*A Week on the Concord*, pp. 113–14).

The passages in which Krishna urges Arjuna to fight do seem to be among the weakest in the poem. For one thing, the logic is faulty:

> These bodies come to an end;
> but that vast embodied Self
> is ageless, fathomless, eternal.
> Therefore you must fight, Arjuna. (2.18)

For another, the means of persuasion include an attempt to shame Arjuna:

> And your enemies will sneer and mock you:
> "The mighty Arjuna, that brave man—
> he slunk from the field like a dog."
> What deeper shame could there be? (2.36)

(The obvious response here would be: "If refusing to fight is the right action, why should I care about the action's fruits or other people's responses?") But above all, the martial rhetoric itself rings hollow, especially in the midst of the glorious cosmic vision of chapter 11:

> Therefore stand up; win glory;
> conquer the enemy; rule. (11.33)

Traditional interpreters of the Gita sometimes justify its imagery by trying to make it into an allegory, in which the battle is an interior battle, Krishna is the Self, Arjuna the ego or the mind, and so forth. But this makes nonsense of the poem. If Arjuna is the mind or ego in every person, what can it possibly mean, for example, to say that he is "born with divine traits" (16.3), whereas other people have "demonic traits"? Who can these others be if Arjuna stands for us all? In fact, the only passages in the poem that give even a hint of an allegorical meaning are 4.42, 8.7, and 18.78.

p. 18 *a buddha enlisting in the war against Hitler*   This buddha would be acting in agreement with the Tao Te Ching, a model of balance and compassion:

> Weapons are the tools of fear;
> a decent man will avoid them
> except in the direst necessity
> and, if compelled, will use them
> only with the utmost restraint.
> Peace is his highest value.
> If the peace has been shattered,
> how can he be content?
> His enemies are not demons,
> but human beings like himself.
> He doesn't wish them personal harm.
> Nor does he rejoice in victory.

How could he rejoice in victory
and delight in the slaughter of men?

He enters a battle gravely,
with sorrow and with great compassion,
as if he were attending a funeral.

(*Tao Te Ching: A New English Version*, chapter 31)

p. 19 *the mature and fully realized "man of yoga"*   The
Gita's portrait of the mature human being is sometimes (especially when it is speaking about nonattachment) equiva-
lent to its portrait of Krishna.

Surrendering all thoughts of outcome,
unperturbed, self-reliant,
he does nothing at all, even
when fully engaged in actions. (4:20)

These actions do not bind me, Arjuna.
I stand apart from them all,
indifferent to their outcome,
unattached, serene. (9.9)

This second quatrain is startlingly reminiscent of one of
the many passages of true spiritual insight from Whitman's
"Song of Myself":

Apart from the pulling and hauling stands what I am,
Stands amused, complacent, compassionating, idle,
      unitary,

Looks down, is erect, bends an arm on an impalpable
    certain rest,
Looks with its sidecurved head, curious what will
    come next,
Both in and out of the game, and watching and
    wondering at it.

(Lines 66–70, 1855 version; section 4, lines 10–14,
1892 version)

p. 21   *"Do your work, then step back"*   *Tao Te Ching:
A New English Version,* chapter 9. This may be a more useful way of saying it, since "renunciation" has such an ascetic tinge to it and makes it seem as if we are giving up
something precious, though in fact what we are giving up is
the cause of great suffering. Both phrases, however, point
to the same truth.

A monk once asked Zen Master Tao-wu, "How can I
keep a clear mind?"

Tao-wu said, "If a thousand people call you and you
don't turn your head, you can say you have achieved
something."

p. 21   *photograph of Ramana Maharshi*   An excellent
reproduction appears on the cover of *The Spiritual Teaching
of Ramana Maharshi* (Shambhala, 1988), well worth the

price of the book, and a much smaller reproduction on the cover of *Be As You Are: The Teachings of Sri Ramana Maharshi* (ed. David Godman, Arkana, 1985), which, however, has a much better selection of teachings.

p. 22 *"When you truly feel equal love for all beings"* *Crumbs from His Table*, Ramanananda Swarnagiri, Sri Ramanasramam, 1969, p. 43.

p. 22 *its chapters about spiritual practice and the sage* Even in these chapters, the Gita contains passages that are culture-bound and should be disregarded by readers who are serious about its deeper teachings. These passages include 1.40–44, 2.2–3, 31–38, 3.10–15, and 8.23–26.

p. 23 *a great philosophical poem* T. S. Eliot, in his 1929 essay on Dante, wrote that as a philosophical poem, the Gita is second only to the Divine Comedy. In terms of artistry, drama, and sheer poetic power, the Divine Comedy is incomparably great, in a category by itself. But the spiritual consciousness that informs it is crude in comparison with the Gita poet's consciousness, not to speak of Lao-tzu's.

p. 28 *"I form the light"* Isaiah 45:7. Compare Blake's marvelous insight from *The Marriage of Heaven and Hell:* "The roaring of lions, the howling of wolves, the raging of the stormy sea, and the destructive sword, are portions of *eternity*, too great for the eye of man."

p. 28 *"The Tao doesn't take sides"* Tao Te Ching: *A New English Version*, chapter 5.

p. 29 *"kind and beautiful"* Gita 11.50.

APPENDIX

The Message of the Gita
by Mohandas K. Gandhi

E ven in 1888 –1889, when I first became acquainted with the Gita, I felt that it was not a historical work, but that under the guise of physical warfare it described the duel that perpetually went on in the hearts of mankind, and that physical warfare was brought in merely to make the description of the internal duel more alluring. This preliminary intuition became more confirmed on a closer study of religion and the Gita. A study of the Mahabharata gave it added confirmation. I do not regard the Mahabharata as a historical work in the accepted sense. The Adiparva contains powerful evidence in support of my opinion. By ascribing to the chief actors superhuman or subhuman origins, the great Vyasa made short work of the history of kings and their peoples. The persons therein described may be historical, but the author of the Mahabharata has used them merely to drive home his religious theme.

The author of the Mahabharata has not established the necessity of physical warfare; on the contrary, he has proved its futility. He has made the victors shed tears of sorrow and repentance, and has left them nothing but a legacy of miseries.

In this great work, the Gita is the crown. Its second chapter, instead of teaching the rules of physical warfare, tells us how a perfected man is to be known. In the characteristics of the perfected man of the Gita, I do not see any to correspond to physical warfare. Its whole design is inconsistent with the rules of conduct governing the relations between warring parties.

Krishna of the Gita is perfection and right knowledge personified, but the picture is imaginary. That does not mean that Krishna, the adored of his people, never lived. But perfection is imagined. The idea of a perfect incarnation is an aftergrowth.

In Hinduism, incarnation is ascribed to one who has performed some extraordinary service to mankind. All embodied life is in reality an incarnation of God, but it is not usual to consider every living being an incarnation. Future generations pay this homage to one who, in his own generation, has been extraordinarily religious in his conduct. I can see nothing wrong in this procedure; it takes nothing from God's greatness, and there is no violence done to truth. There is an Urdu saying that means "Adam is not God, but he is a spark of the Divine." And therefore he who is the most religiously behaved has most of the divine spark in him. It is in accordance with this train of thought that Krishna enjoys in Hinduism the status of the most perfect incarnation.

This belief in incarnation is a testimony to man's lofty spiritual ambition. Man is not at peace with himself till he has become like God. The endeavor to reach this state is the supreme, the only, ambition worth having. And this is self-realization. This self-realization is the subject of the Gita, as it is of all scriptures. But its author surely did not write it to establish that doctrine. The object of the Gita appears to me to be that of showing the most excellent way to attain self-realization. That which is to be found, more or less clearly, spread out here and there in Hindu religious books, has been brought out in the clearest possible language in the Gita, even at the risk of repetition.

That matchless remedy is renunciation of the fruits of action.

This is the center around which the Gita is woven. This renunciation is the central sun around which devotion, knowledge, and the rest revolve like planets. The body has been likened to a prison. There must be action where there is a body. Not one embodied being is exempted from action. And yet all religions proclaim that it is possible for man, by treating the body as the temple of God, to attain freedom. How can the body be made the temple of God? In other words, how can one be free from action, i.e., from the taint of sin? The Gita has answered the question in decisive language: "By desireless action; by renouncing the fruits of action; by dedicating all activities to God, i.e., by surrendering oneself to Him body and soul."

But desirelessness or renunciation does not come by merely talking about it. It is not attained by an intellectual feat. It is attainable only by a constant heart-churn. Right knowledge is necessary for attaining renunciation. Learned men possess a knowledge of a kind. They may recite the Vedas from memory, yet they may be steeped in self-indulgence. In order that knowledge may not run riot, the author of the Gita has insisted on devotion accompanying it and has given devotion the first place. Knowledge without devotion will be like a misfire. "Therefore," says the Gita, "have devotion, and knowledge will follow." This devotion is not mere lip-worship, it is wrestling with death. Hence the Gita's assessment of the devotee's qualities is similar to that of the sage's.

Thus the devotion required by the Gita is no softhearted effusiveness. It certainly is not blind faith. The devotion of the Gita has the least to do with externals. A devotee may use, if he likes, rosaries, forehead marks, make offerings, but these things are no test of his devotion. He is a true devotee who is jealous of no one, who is a fount of mercy, who is without egotism, who is selfless, who treats alike cold and heat, happiness and misery, who is always forgiving, who is always contented, whose resolutions are firm, who has dedicated mind and soul to God, who causes no dread, who is not afraid of others, who is free from exultation, sorrow, and fear, who is pure, who is versed in action and yet remains unaffected by it, who renounces all fruits of action, good or bad, who treats friend and enemy alike, who is untouched by respect or disrespect, who is not puffed up by praise, who does not go under when people speak ill of him, who loves silence and solitude, who has a disciplined mind. Such devotion is inconsistent with the existence at the same time of strong attachments.

We thus see that to be a real devotee is to realize oneself. Self-realization is not something apart. One rupee can purchase for us poison or nectar, but knowledge or devotion cannot buy us either salvation or bondage. These are themselves the things we want. In other words, if the means and the end are not identical, they are almost identical. The extreme of means is salvation. The salvation of the Gita is perfect peace.

But such knowledge and devotion, to be true, have to stand the test of renunciation of the fruits of action. Mere knowledge of right and wrong will not make one fit for salvation. According to common notions, a mere learned man will pass as a *pandit* [scholar]. He need not perform any service. He will regard it as bondage even to lift a little *lota* [water pot]. Where one test of knowledge is nonliability for service, there is no room for such mundane work as the lifting of a *lota*.

Or take *bhakti* [devotion]. The popular notion of *bhakti* is softheartedness, counting beads and the like, and disdaining to do even a loving service, lest the counting of beads, etc., might be interrupted. This *bhakta* [devotee] therefore leaves the rosary only for eating, drinking, and the like, never for grinding corn or nursing patients.

But the Gita says, "No one has attained his goal without action. Even men like Janaka attained salvation through action. If ever I were to cease working, the world would perish. How much more necessary then it is for the people at large to engage in action."

While on the one hand it is beyond dispute that all action binds, on the other hand it is equally true that all living beings have to do some work whether they wish to or not. Here all activity, whether mental or physical, is to be included in the term "action." Then how is one to be free from the bondage of action, even though he may be acting? The manner in which the Gita has solved the problem is, to my knowledge, unique. The Gita says, "Do your allotted work but renounce its fruit — be detached and act — have no desire for reward, and act."

This is the unmistakable teaching of the Gita. He who gives up action, falls. He who gives up only the reward, rises. But renunciation of fruit in no way means indifference to the result. In regard to every action one must know the result that is expected to follow, the means thereto, and the capacity for it. He who, being thus equipped, is without desire for the result, and is yet wholly engrossed in the due fulfillment of the task before him, is said to have renounced the fruits of his action.

Again, let no one consider renunciation to mean lack of fruit for the renouncer. The Gita reading does not warrant such a meaning. Renunciation means absence of hankering after fruit. As a matter of fact, he who renounces reaps a thousandfold. The renunciation of the Gita is the acid test of faith. He who is always brooding over results often loses nerve in the performance of his duty. He becomes impatient and then gives vent to anger and begins to do unworthy things; he jumps from action to action, never remaining faithful to any. He who broods over results is like a man given to objects of the senses: he is always distracted, he says good-bye to all scruples, everything is right in his estimation, and he therefore resorts to means fair and foul to attain his end.

From the bitter experiences of desire for fruit, the author of the Gita discovered the path of renunciation of fruit, and put it before the world in a most convincing manner. The common belief is that religion is always opposed to material good. "One cannot act religiously in mercantile and other such matters, there is no place for religion in such pursuits, religion is only for attainment of salvation," we hear many worldly-wise people say. In my opinion the author of the Gita has dispelled this delusion. He has drawn no line of demarcation between salvation and worldly pursuits. On the contrary, he has shown that religion must rule even our worldly pursuits. I have felt that the Gita teaches us that what cannot be followed in our day-to-day practice cannot be called religion. Thus, according to the Gita, all acts that are incapable of being performed without attachment are taboo. This golden rule saves mankind from many a pitfall. According to this interpretation, murder, lying, dissoluteness, and the like must be regarded as sinful and therefore taboo. Man's life then becomes simple, and from that simplicity peace arises.

Thinking along these lines, I have felt that in trying to enforce in one's life the central teaching of the Gita, one is bound to follow truth and *ahimsa* [nonviolence]. When there is no desire for fruit, there is no temptation for untruth or *himsa* [violence]. Take any instance of untruth or violence, and it will be found that behind it was the desire to attain the cherished end. But it may be freely admitted that the Gita was not written to establish *ahimsa*. That was an accepted and primary duty even before the time of the Gita. The Gita had to deliver the message of the renunciation of fruit. This is clearly brought out as early as the second chapter.

But if the Gita believed in *ahimsa* or it was included in desirelessness, why did the author adopt a warlike illustration? When the Gita was written, although people believed in *ahimsa*, wars were not only not taboo, but no one observed the contradiction between them and *ahimsa*.

In assessing the implications of the renunciation of fruit, we are not required to probe the mind of the author of the Gita as to his limitations of *ahimsa* and the like. Because a poet presented a particular truth to the world, it does not necessarily follow that he has known or worked out all its great consequences, or that having done so he is always able to express them fully. In this, perhaps, lies the greatness of the poem and the poet. A poet's meaning is limitless. Like man, the meaning of great writings undergoes evolution. On examining the history of languages, we notice that the meaning of important words has changed or expanded. This is true of the Gita. The author has himself extended the meanings of some of the current words. We are able to discover this even on a superficial examination. It is possible that in the age prior to that of the Gita, offering of animals in sacrifice was permissible. But there is not a trace of it in the word *yajña* [sacrifice or worship] in the Gita's sense. In the Gita, continuous concentration on God is the king of sacrifices. The third chapter seems to show that sacrifice chiefly means body labor for service. The third and fourth chapters read together will give us other meanings for sacrifice, but never animal sacrifice. Similarly, the meaning of the word *sannyasa* [renunciation] has undergone a transformation in the Gita. The *sannyasa* of the Gita will not tolerate complete cessation of all activity. The *sannyasa* of the Gita is all work and yet not work. Thus the author of the Gita, by extending the meanings of words, has taught us to imitate him. Let it be granted that, according to the letter of the Gita, it is possible to say that warfare is consistent with the renunciation of fruit. But after forty years' unremitting endeavor fully to enforce the teaching of the Gita in my own life, I have in all humility felt that perfect renunciation is impossible without perfect observance of *ahimsa* in every shape and form.

The Gita is not an aphoristic work, it is a great religious poem. The deeper you dive into it, the richer the meanings you get. Since it is meant for the people at large, there is pleasing repetition. With every age the important words will carry new and expanding meanings. But its central teaching will never vary. The seeker is at liberty to extract from this treasure any meaning he likes so as to enable him to enforce in his life the central teaching.

Nor is the Gita a collection of dos and don'ts. What is lawful for one may be unlawful for another. What may be permissible at one time, or in one place, may not be so at another time and in another place. Desire for fruit is the only universal prohibition. Desirelessness is obligatory.

The Gita has sung the praises of knowledge, but it is beyond the mere intellect, it is essentially addressed to the heart and capable of being understood by the heart. Therefore the Gita is not for those who have no faith. The author makes Krishna say, "Do not entrust this treasure to him who is without sacrifice, without emotion, without the desire for this teaching and who denies Me. On the other hand, those who will give this precious treasure to My devotees will by the fact of this service assuredly reach Me. And those who, being free from malice, will with faith absorb this teaching, shall, having attained freedom, live where people of true merit go after death."

Acknowledgments

I would like to express my gratitude to Michael Katz, my agent; Peter Guzzardi, my editor; and Linda Loewenthal, my publisher; to Katherine Beitner, Tina Constable, Debbie Koenig, Liz Matthews, Mary Schuck, Barbara Sturman, and Jim Walsh of Harmony Books; to Elaine Pagels and John Tarrant for their useful suggestions; to the Lyndhurst Foundation for a prize that helped support my work; and, most of all, to Vicki.

FROM BESTSELLING AUTHOR AND
TRANSLATOR STEPHEN MITCHELL

THE FROG PRINCE
0-609-60545-3
$18.00 hardcover
(Canada: $27.50)

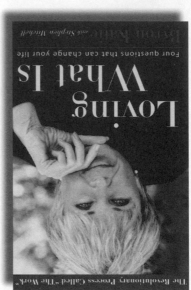

ALSO
RECOMMENDED

LOVING WHAT IS
Byron Katie
with Stephen Mitchell
0-609-60874-6
$24.00 hardcover
(Canada: $36.00)
(Available in paperback
from Three Rivers Press
in Spring 2003)